Praise for the Weird & Wacky Holiday Marketing Guide through the years ...

"The marketing ideas that this book provides make it worth every penny! I love this guide. I recently bought this book because I was looking for unique ways to market my business. The guide is an excellent resource for planning current and future advertising campaigns and marketing events, and I was amazed to learn how many planned commemorations there are in the United States and around the world that I could take advantage of. Because the book is organized by day, month, and year, it gives me a comprehensive way to plan our marketing. The creative marketing ideas that the author offers makes the price of the book worth every cent!"
Jay Lynch (2018 Edition)

"A Google Search on Steroids! Have you ever done a Google search while preparing a presentation and found an incredible list that helped you add lots of ideas to what you were doing? I have and know that having such a list always gives me lots of information to make my presentation more interesting and colorful.

"Ginger Marks' 2018 Weird & Wacky Holiday Marketing Guide is just like having the results of a Google search, only it is like having such a list on steroids! The guide contains an overwhelming number of marketing ideas. The first 70 pages list national, international, and quite frankly, often quirky and humorous events which take place throughout the year, listed in month-to-month order. If humor is what you are looking for, you will learn that National Hermit Week falls in June, "Hot Enough for Ya Day" falls on July 23rd, and August 7th is known as the "Particularly Preposterous Packaging Day." These three dates are just samples of the hundreds (even maybe a thousand) of weird and wacky celebrations, festivals, and events that are included in Ginger Marks' 2018 guide.

"The second half of the book contains several appendices, which once again provides all kinds of marketing information. I can't imagine a business owner who couldn't find some great marketing ideas while looking through the first half of this book, or who *couldn't find links to companies that might help his or her business in the second half of the book. There is so much information here. The 2018 Weird & Wacky Holiday Marketing Guide is a terrific resource!"*

Gary Ciesla (2018 Edition)

"People love to buy. They especially love to buy when they have a reason. The **Holiday Marketing Guide** *provides clever marketing strategies to increase sales every month of the year based on events and holidays. It's a brilliant guide for the savvy marketer."*

Daniel Hall, Creator of *Free Marketing Tutorials* **at DanielHallPresents.com (2016 Edition)**

"Ginger Marks has put together a fantastic resource! If you are looking for outside of the box ideas for marketing as well as for celebrating, you are going to love the Weird & Wacky Holiday Marketing Guide. As a former elementary school teacher, I wish I had had a copy of this incredible resource when I was teaching. The month-long and week-long holidays, listed throughout this guide, could create the foundation for exciting study units."

D'vorah Lansky, M.Ed. Best-Selling author of *Book Marketing Made Easy,* **www.BookMarketingMadeEasy.com (2016 Edition)**

"Great marketing tools for social media business exposure Having multiple businesses and also doing websites, I found this book to be a wonderful asset for trying to come up with new "and different" ideas for marketing, especially on social media. Talk about having every holiday imaginable listed in this book!! there are also so many that it intrigues your interest to go off & further investigate on your own, after learning about them for the first time.

"I personally liked that at the end of the calendar month she adds some ideas on how to use these holidays to your advantage in marketing, but more importantly, she is always adding comments that you can raise the money for charity or a good cause (not just to market your business but also help your community at the same time). If you have a business that is seeking attention on social media, I think this book will help you announce some totally weird & wacky facts for every day of the year, that will certainly get you noticed!! A wealth of resources here."

Cheryl (2018 Edition)

"So much info in one book! As a business owner, it's difficult to stand out. With Ginger's guidance you can set yourself apart from the crowd. It's well-written and easy to follow. Tons and tons of info and well worth it!"

Patti Knoles, Virtual Graphic Arts Department (2017 Edition)

"Awesome very practical and fun marketing ideas. Ginger Marks' 2018 Weird and Wacky Holiday Marketing Guide is an amazing book and tool for me to use preparing speeches in my business. Using anecdotes from the book I can enhance my presentations to be much more fun and colorful and keep the audience entertained. I can't wait to show this book to my colleagues.

"There are numerous marketing ideas I never would have come up with on my own that I plan to use in my business social media which should really help engagement. I love that I can get new ideas all year long!"

Rachel I (2018 Edition)

2019 Weird & Wacky Holiday Marketing Guide
11th Edition

Your business marketing calendar of ideas

Ginger Marks

DocUmeant *Publishing*
244 5th Avenue
Suite G-200
NY, NY 10001
646-233-4366
www.DocUmeantPublishing.com

Volume 11 First Edition, December 2018

Published by DocUmeant Publishing
244 5th Ave, Ste G–200
NY, NY 10001
646-233-4366

©Copyright 2019 Ginger Marks All rights reserved. No portion of this book may be duplicated in any way by any means, electronically or manually without the expressed written permission of the author, except for personal use. Address all comments and questions to Ginger.Marks@DocUmeantDesigns.com.

Editor Wendy VanHatten
VanHatten Writing Services
www.wendyvanhatten.com

Layout and Design Ginger Marks
DocUmeant Designs
www.DocUmeantDesigns.com

Library of Congress: 2018914524

ISBN: 978-1-9378-0197-7 (print)

Contents

Praise for the Weird & Wacky Holiday Marketing Guide through the years ...- - -a

Introduction -1

Annual Dates of Note -3
    International Year of the Periodic Table of Chemical Elements 3
    International Year of Indigenous Language 4
    United Nations International Year of Moderation 4
    Chinese Year of the Pig 4
        Strengths 5
        Matches 5
        Pig's Personality by Blood Type 5

JANUARY -7
    MONTH-LONG HOLIDAYS 7
    WEEK-LONG HOLIDAYS 7
    DAILY HOLIDAYS 7
    HOLIDAY MARKETING IDEAS FOR JANUARY 9

FEBRUARY -11
    MONTH-LONG HOLIDAYS 11
    WEEK-LONG HOLIDAYS 11
    DAILY HOLIDAYS 11
    HOLIDAY MARKETING IDEAS FOR FEBRUARY 13

MARCH -16
    MONTH-LONG HOLIDAYS 16
    WEEK-LONG HOLIDAYS 16
    DAILY HOLIDAYS 17
    HOLIDAY MARKETING IDEAS FOR MARCH 19

APRIL -21
    MONTH-LONG HOLIDAYS 21
    WEEK-LONG HOLIDAYS 21
    DAILY HOLIDAYS 22
    HOLIDAY MARKETING IDEAS FOR APRIL 24

MAY -27
    MONTH-LONG HOLIDAYS 27
    WEEK-LONG HOLIDAYS 27
    DAILY HOLIDAYS 28
    HOLIDAY MARKETING IDEAS FOR MAY 30

JUNE --**32**
    MONTH-LONG HOLIDAYS 32
    WEEK-LONG HOLIDAYS 32
    DAILY HOLIDAYS 32
    HOLIDAY MARKETING IDEAS FOR JUNE 34

JULY ---**37**
    MONTH-LONG HOLIDAYS 37
    WEEK-LONG HOLIDAYS 37
    DAILY HOLIDAYS 37
    HOLIDAY MARKETING IDEAS FOR JULY 39

AUGUST --**41**
    MONTH-LONG HOLIDAYS 41
    WEEK-LONG HOLIDAYS 41
    DAILY HOLIDAYS 42
    HOLIDAY MARKETING IDEAS FOR AUGUST 44

SEPTEMBER --**47**
    MONTH-LONG HOLIDAYS 47
    WEEK-LONG HOLIDAYS 47
    DAILY HOLIDAYS 48
    HOLIDAY MARKETING IDEAS FOR SEPTEMBER 50

OCTOBER --**52**
    MONTH-LONG HOLIDAYS 52
    WEEK-LONG HOLIDAYS 52
    DAILY HOLIDAYS 53
    HOLIDAY MARKETING IDEAS FOR OCTOBER 55

NOVEMBER ---**57**
    MONTH-LONG HOLIDAYS 57
    WEEK-LONG HOLIDAYS 57
    DAILY HOLIDAYS 57
    HOLIDAY MARKETING IDEAS FOR NOVEMBER 59

DECEMBER ---**62**
    MONTH-LONG HOLIDAYS 62
    WEEK-LONG HOLIDAYS 62
    DAILY HOLIDAYS 62
    HOLIDAY MARKETING IDEAS FOR DECEMBER 64

Appendix A: SAMPLES --**67**
    Sample Press Release 67
    Pop Music Day Artist/Song Titles 68
    Pop Music Song Cryptograms 70
    Name This Artist 71
    Podcast Directory 73
    Judgment Day Card 74
    Croissant Day Recipes 75

| v

Croissant Day Card 82
National Broken Heart Day Fact Sheet 84
How To Organize a Drive 85
    Timeline: 86
Sample Financial Gift Form 88
Foster Parent Facts 89
    What Are the Requirements To Be a Foster Parent? 89
Freedom Day Social Media Image 92
Random Acts of Kindness Cards 93
Polar Bear Fun Fact Sheet 94
Polar Bear Flyer 95
Fun Facts About Name Day Graphics 96
90+ Twitter Tools 97
    Analytics 97
    Chat 98
    Discovery 98
    Follow/Unfollow 99
    Hashtags 99
    Images 100
    Mentioning & Monitoring 100
    Scheduling 101
    Timing 101
    Trending 101
    Top Clients 101
    Miscellaneous Tools 102
Twitter Tips 104
Holy Humor Month Jokes 105
National Beer Day Graphic 106
World Penguin Day Fun Facts 107
National Baby Sitters Day Emergency Contacts 108
Supply Chain Professionals Day Graphic 109
National Eat at a Food Truck Day Card 110
Food Truck Tweets 111
Medical Information Card 112
Tell an Old Joke Day Graphic 113
Pirate Event Poster 114
International Wave at Surveillance Day Graphic 115
Earth Hour Day Event Flyer 116
Positive Attitude Month Quotes 117
National Taco Day Coloring Page 119
Hockey Mask Day Template 120
Area Code Day Graphic 121
Lighten Up Loosen Up Day Graphic 122
Name Your PC Day Graphic 124
Freedom from Slavery Event Poster 125
National Fire Safety Counsel Day Graphic 126
Festivus Day Quotes 127
    Customer Service 127

Conflict	127
Festivus Day Graphic	129

Appendix B: 2019 Social Media Image Size Guide — 131

Facebook	131
LinkedIn	131
YouTube	132
Instagram	132
Twitter	132
Pinterest	133
Tumbler	133
Google+	133
Ello	134
SnapChat	134
Chinese Social Media	134
WeChat	134
Weibo	135

Appendix C: LINKS — 137

Link Checker	137
Auto Responder Services	137
Books and Movies	137
Greeting Card Companies	138
Podcast Directories	138
Promotional Product Supply Companies	138
Quote Sources	139
Stock Photos	139
Teleconference Companies	140
Virtual Assistant Companies	140
Webinar Services	140

Appendix D: RESOURCES — 143

Twitter Tools Resources	143
Analytics	143
Chat	143
Discovery	143
Follow/Unfollow	144
Hashtags	144
Images	144
Mentioning & Monitoring	144
Scheduling	144
Timing	145
Trending	145
Top Clients	145
Miscellaneous Tools	145

About the Author — 147

Additional Works by Ginger Marks — 149

Introduction

Events are one of the smartest prescriptions for slumping sales and for maintaining a healthy business. It's not enough anymore to merely have goods on the shelf and open the doors on time every day. We all need to reinvent our businesses to keep them thriving and healthy. And, that is just what this book helps you achieve.

This unique marketing book continues to win awards year after year and remains a #1 Best-Seller in the Business Marketing genre. Highly praised by marketing experts and now entering its second decade, this book offers more fun and easy marketing ideas exclusively penned for the calendar year 2019. Now you can grow your business with strategies built around wacky holidays, observed throughout the world, for the entire 2019 calendar year. If you missed the premier 2009 issue or want to complete your collection, all previous and unique yearly editions are available at http://www.HolidayMarketingGuide.com.

As *Weird & Wacky Holiday Marketing Guide* is read and used internationally, I have included many International holidays.

To take advantage of the information provided, pick a day and discover the unusual holidays celebrated on that date. Then, read the corresponding month's "Holiday Marketing Ideas" section to find a simple implementation or allow it to open your creative mind and think of some of your own.

Please note that the asterisk (*) in front of a holiday means a specific holiday is celebrated on that numerical date each year. For example, Christmas Day is December 25 no matter what day that falls on during the calendar week.

Here's another exceptional marketing idea for you I discovered when visiting BrownieLocks.com back in 2009, and which is now listed in the official *Chase Calendar of Events* which I cull from every year. Bonza Bottler Days™—the day is the same as the month it is in. That equates to: 1/1, 2/2, 3/3, etc. There is one in every month. There you have it; another extra fine excuse for an event to boost your notoriety and sales each and every month!

This is by no means a comprehensive edition. I have made all attempts to ensure the accuracy of the contents. If you encounter errors or know of a holiday that needs to be included, please let me know so they can be addressed in future editions. But remember, if your suggested holiday addition is not listed in the official *Chase Calendar of Events* it is not eligible for inclusion.

Read on, have fun, initiate your own version of these holidays, and reap the benefit for your business.

Ginger Marks

P.S. I have included a new appendix section titled, "2018 Social Media Image Size Guide" to simplify your Weird & Wacky Holiday Marketing social media image creation. Look for it in the appendix section. You'll probably refer to it often enough to necessitate making a copy and keep handy.

P.S.S. The *Weird & Wacky Holiday Marketing Companion Playbook*. This tool is intended to help you to create, organize, and put the FUN back into your marketing plan. Each monthly calendar offers space for you to begin your planning and keep all your notes in one handy book. Since each year the physical calendar days rotate, I have left the date numbers blank to enable you to make use of this *Companion Playbook* beginning today.

Annual Dates of Note

International Year of the Periodic Table of Chemical Elements

To coincide with the 150th anniversary of the discovery of the Periodic System by Russian scientist, Dmitry Mendeleev, a father of modern chemistry, the UN has proclaimed 2019 as the International Year of the Periodic Table of Chemical Elements (IYPTCE). Mendeleev's defining 1869 breakthrough was the prediction of properties of five elements and their compounds; he also left space in the Periodic Table for elements to be discovered in the future. The Periodic Table, a unique tool enabling scientists the predict the appearance and properties of matter on Earth and in the universe, is an example of science's global language, with broad implications in astronomy, chemistry, physics, biology, and other natural sciences.

SCIENCE – SOCIETY – WORLD – SUSTAINABLE DEVELOPMENT

Administered by UNESCO and the International Union of Pure and Applied Chemistry, IYPTCE is a recognition of the important role of the basic sciences, especially chemistry and physics, while also paying tribute to the recent discovering and naming of four super-heavy elements of the Periodic Table with the atomic numbers 113 (Nihonium), 115 (Moscovium),

117 (Tennessine), and 118 (Oganesson) resulting from close international scientific cooperation. The opening ceremony kicks off the year Jan 29 at UNESCO Headquarters, Paris. A symposium, "The Periodic Table at 150" during IUPAC's centenary coincides with a celebration of the 150th anniversary of Mendeleev's Periodic Table during the 47th World Chemistry Congress in Paris in July. Additional commemorations will take place at the Mendeleev International Chemistry Olympiad (Paris, April); the Markovnikov Congress (June); the International Chemistry Olympiad (Paris, July); the EuCheMs Inorganic Chemistry Conference (Greece, June); and the jubilee Mendeleev Congress on General and Applied Chemistry (St. Petersburg, September). For more information: www.iypt2019.org.

International Year of Indigenous Language

As part of a 2017 resolution on the rights of the world's indigenous peoples, the UN General Assembly proclaimed 2019 as the International Year of Indigenous Languages, a year-long series of action-oriented activities focusing on "the critical risks confronting indigenous languages and the significance of such risks for sustainable development, reconciliation, good governance, and peace building." Language in general plays a crucial role in people's identity, social integration and development, while indigenous languages in particular impact a wide range of indigenous issues including education, scientific and technological development, biosphere and the environment, freedom of expression, employment and social inclusion. Per UNESCO, 90 percent of the world's languages could disappear before 2099.

With UNESCO serving as the lead agency, the International Year unites educators, governments, activists, cultural organizations, athletes and goodwill ambassadors to coordinate events, curricula and initiatives to celebrate more than 7,000 languages still spoken. The International Year website showcases communication campaigns, documentary shorts, and a calendar of events including exhibitions, concerts, film festivals, and sports and game festivals, including the launch event at UNESCO headquarters in Paris and the biannual World Indigenous Nations Games. For more information: https://en.unesco.org/IY2019.

United Nations International Year of Moderation

Recognizing that moderation is an important value and approach to countering violent extremism as and when conducive to terrorism and to promoting dialogue, mutual respect and understanding, and that moderation can reinforce the advancement of the three pillars of the United Nations: peace and security, development and human rights, the general Assembly in Resolution 72/129 on Dec 8, 2017, declared 2019 as the International Year of Moderation. For more information: www.un.org.

Chinese Year of the Pig[1]

Dog is the twelfth in the 12-year cycle of Chinese zodiac sign. The Years of the Pig include 1923, 1935, 1947, 1959, 1971, 1983, 1995, 2007, 2019, 2031, 2043 . . . Pig is not thought to be a smart animal in China. It likes sleeping and eating and becomes fat. Thus, it usually features laziness

---

[1] Travel China Guide. http://www.travelchinaguide.com/intro/social_customs/zodiac/pig.htm.

and clumsiness. On the positive side, it behaves itself, has no plan to harm others, and can bring affluence to people. Consequently, it has been regarded as wealth.

People with Chinese zodiac Pig sign are considerate, responsible, independent and optimistic. They always show generousness and mercy to endure other people's mistakes, which help them gain harmonious interpersonal relationships. However, sometimes they will behave lazy and lack actions. In addition, pure hearts would let them be cheated easily in daily life.

Lucky Numbers: 2, 5, 8

Lucky Colors: yellow, grey, brown, gold

Lucky Flowers: hydrangea, pitcher plant, marguerite

Lucky Directions: southeast, northeast

Strengths
Warm-hearted, good-tempered, loyal, honest, gentle
Weaknesses
Naive, gullible, sluggish, short-tempered

Matches
Perfect: Tiger, Rabbit, Sheep
These combinations always have a high possibility to obtain a sweet and everlasting marriage. When meeting difficulties, they can face them together. More patience and enough encouragement are keys to solve problems. They have common goals and similar values, which add more fun in daily life.

Avoid: Snake, Monkey
Totally different personalities may lead to conflicts. They always have completely contrary opinions about one thing and cannot reach an agreement because of their stubbornness. If getting married, one would always think about his/her own advantages and feelings, which would hurt the other.

Pig's Personality by Blood Type
Blood Type O: They are brave and full of enthusiasm. Most of them are independent. They believe that success should be achieved by own efforts.

Blood Type A: Their gentle and optimistic characteristics can always influence people around. They are reliable, and always try their best to help friends who are in trouble.

Blood Type B: In most cases, they are honest to everyone, which gives enough sense of security to their partners.

Blood Type AB: They have high responsibility towards career, with enviable intelligence and outstanding abilities. They are born leaders that can make full use of everyone's advantages.

JANUARY

MONTH-LONG HOLIDAYS

Jan 6 – Mar 5 Carnival Season

Be Kind to Food Servers Month, Book Blitz Month, Children Impacted by a Parent's Cancer Month, Clap4Health Month, Get Organized Month, International Brain Teaser Month, International Child-Centered Divorce Month, International Creativity Month, National Clean Up Your Computer Month, National Glaucoma Awareness Month, National Hot Tea Month, National Mentoring Month, National Personal Self-Defense Awareness Month, National Poverty in America Awareness Month, National Radon Action Month, National Skating Month, National Slavery and Human Trafficking Prevention Month, National Volunteer Blood Donor Month, Oatmeal Month, Worldwide Rising Star Month

WEEK-LONG HOLIDAYS

Jan 1 – 2 Taiwan: Foundation Days
Jan 1 – 3 Japanese Era New Year
Jan 2 – 8 Someday We'll Laugh about This Week
Jan 7 – 9 Elvis Presley Birthday Celebration
Jan 8 – 14 Dating and Life Coach Recognition Week
Jan 11-17 Cuckoo Dancing Week
Jan 16 – 20 Career Builder Challenge
Jan 18 – 25 Week of Christian Unity
Jan 19 – 20 Bald Eagle Appreciation Days
Jan 20 – 26 Clean Out Your Inbox Week
Jan 27 – Feb 2 Catholic Schools Week

DAILY HOLIDAYS

1. Betsy Ross Birthday (1752), *Bonza Bottler Day™, Canada: Polar Bear Swim, *Copyright Revision Law Signed (1976), Cuba: Liberation Day and 60th Anniversary of the Revolution, Czech–Slovak Divorce (1993; Anniversary of separation into two nations), *Ellis Island Opened Anniversary (1892), *Emancipation Proclamation (1863), *Euro Introduced (1999), *First Baby Boomer Born–Kathleen Casey Wilkens in Philadelphia, PA (1946), *Frankenstein Published (200th Anniversary), *Haiti: Independence Day, *Mummer's Parade, *National Environmental Policy Act (1970), *New Year's Day, *New Year's Dishonor List Day, *Paul Revere Birthday (1735), Russia: New Year's Day Observance, Saint Basil's Day, Stock Exchange Holiday, Sudan: Independence Day, *Z–Day
2. 55 MPH Speed Limit Day (1974), Haiti: Ancestor's Day, *Happy Mew Year for Cats Day, Japan: Kakizome, Switzerland: Berchtoldstag

3. *Alaska Admission Day, Congress Assembles, *Drinking Straw Day (1888), Earth at Perihelion, J.R.R. Tolkien Birthday Anniversary (1892), Memento Mori Day, Saint Genevieve Day
4. *Amnesty for Polygamists: Anniversary (1893), *Dimpled Chad Day, *Elizabeth Ann Bayley–Seton Feast Day, *Myanmar Independence Day, *Pop Music Chart Day, Sir Isaac Newton Birthday (1643), *Trivia Day, Utah: Admission Day (1896), *World Braille Day, World's Tallest Building Day
5. *Alvin Ailey (1931), *Five-Dollar-a-Day Minimum Wage Day (1914), National Bird Day, Twelfth Night
6. *Armenian Christmas, *Epiphany or Twelfth Day, Italy: La Befana, New Mexico: Admission Day (1912), Pan Am Circles Earth (1942), *Three Kings Day
7. England: Plough Monday, *First Balloon Fight Across English Channel (1785), *Harlem Globetrotter's Day, *International Programmers' Day, Japan: Nanakusa and Usokae, National Thank God It's Monday! Day, Orthodox Christmas, Trans-Atlantic Phoning (1927)
8. Argyle Day, Greece: Midwife's Day or Women's Day, *Elvis Presley Birth (1935), *National Joygerm Day, Poetry at Work Day, *Show and Tell Day at Work, *War on Poverty Day (1964)
9. *Aviation in America Day (1793), *Panama's Martyr Day
10. League of Nations Founding (1946)
11. Learn Your Name in Morse Code Day, Morocco: Independence Day, Nepal: National Unity Day, US Surgeon General Declares Cigarettes Hazardous (1964)
12. *Haiti Earthquake Day (2010), National Hot Yea Day
13. Norway: Tyvendedagen, *Radio Broadcasting Day, Russia: Old New Year's Eve, Sweden: Saint Knut's Day, Switzerland: Meitlisunntig, Togo: Liberation Day
14. *Benedict Arnold Day, Caesarean Section Day (1794), National Clean Off Your Desk Day, *Ratification Day
15. Alpha Kappa Alpha Fororrity Day (1908), Martin Luther King Birthday (1929), Molière Day, National Bagel Day, Quarterly Estimated Federal Income Tax Payers' Due Date (also Apr 15, Jun 17 and Sep 16, 2018)
16. *Appreciate a Dragon Day, *Civil Service Day, El Salvador: National Day of Peace, Japan: Haru-No-Yabuiri, *National Nothing Day, National Quinoa Day, *Religious Freedom Day
17. *Al Capone Day, *Ben Franklin Birthday (1706), *Cable Car Day, Get to Know Your Customers Day (also April 18, July 18, and Oct 17, set aside to get to know your customers even better), International Mentoring Day, *Judgment Day, Kid Inventors' Day, Mexico: Blessing of the Animals at the Cathedral, Poland: Liberation Day, Popeye Day (90th Anniversary, 1929), Saint Anthony's Day, Southern California Earthquake Day
18. Arbor Day in Florida, Daniel Webster Day, International Fetish Day, *Louis and Clark Expedition Commissioned (1803), *Pooh Day
19. *Confederate Heroes Day (Texas), Ethiopia: Timket, National Popcorn Day, Poe Day
20. Brazil: San Sebastian's Day, Guinea-Bissau: National Heroes Day, Lesotho: Army Day, Stephen Foster Day
21. First Concorde Flight, Kiwanis International: Anniversary, ML King, Jr Day, *National Hugging Day™, Tu B'Shvat
22. *Answer Your Cat's Questions Day, *Roe vs. Wade Day, *Saint Vincent Feast Day, Ukraine: Ukrainian Day
23. Bulgaria: Babin Den, *National Handwriting Day, Snowplow Mailbox Hockey Day
24. *Belly Laugh Day, *Beer Can Day, *National Compliment Day

25. *A Room of One's Own Day, *Around the World in 72 Days Day, First Scheduled Transcontinental Flight, *Macintosh Computer Day (1984), National Preschool Fitness Day, Saint Dwynwen Day
26. Australia: Australia Day, Dental Drill Day, Dominican Republic: National Holiday, Eagle Days, India: Republic Day, Indian Earthquake, Local Quilt Shop Day, National Seed Swap Day
27. Apollo I: Spacecraft Fire (1967), Germany: Day of Remembrance for Victims of Nazism, *Mozart Day, National Geographic Society Day, *Thomas Crapper Day, United Nations: International Day of Commemoration in Memory of the Victims of the Holocaust, *Viet Nam Peace Day, World Leprosy Day
28. Bubble Wrap Appreciation Day, *Challenger Space Shuttle Explosion (1986), Data Privacy Day
29. *Curmudgeons Day, Scotland: Up Helly AA Day, *Seeing Eye Dog Day
30. Bloody Sunday, Inane Answering Message Day, Jordan: King's Birthday, National Croissant Day, Tet Offensive Begins: 50th Anniversary
31. *First Social Security Check Issued Day, *Inspire Your Heart with Art Day, Nauru: National Holiday, Schubert Day

HOLIDAY MARKETING IDEAS FOR JANUARY

International Creativity Month — Let your creativity soar this month! Creativity is vital to the health of your business and that's what the *Weird & Wacky Holiday Marketing Guide* is all about. So, it should not be surprising to you that I am focusing on this weird and wacky holiday. Gather a group of like-minded business owners to discover a fresh new way to problem-solve or innovate. If nothing else, it will revitalize your confidence.

To take it one step further than joining or forming a mastermind group, another fun way to celebrate this month is with hand-drawn or home-made greeting or note cards. Send a few out to your customers or clients to let them know you are thinking about them. Sometimes it's that little spark that lights a fire in their mind reminding them of their need to purchase from or hire you.

Jan 4 Pop Music Chart Day — One fun activity for today is to celebrate with games. Cryptograms of best-selling pop songs, name that tune games, which is one that can be easily done online, or name that artist too would work. When you host a game day, you'll capture the attention of those who may not even have heard of you before.

To keep it simple you might celebrate by posting on social media some pop song lyrics that relate to your business. As an example, if you sell candles you could use the lyrics to "Light My Fire" by the Doors (does that date me? wink). If you sell spices, like my good friend, Ms. Bea of Sage Hill Farms, you might use Elvis Presley's "Shake, Rattle, and Roll". Even Christian based businesses have top Christian artists and songs that you can use. So, as you can easily see, this weird and wacky holiday can be used even by you!

You'll find a few titles through the ages and even some games in the Sample appendix to get you started.

Jan 13 Radio Broadcasting Day—What better day to promote your business than today. We all know how podcasts and traditional radio can help get the word out about your business. So, if you can schedule an appearance take advantage of that opportunity. If, however, you want to get your name out there and keep it there—but you aren't up to starting your own show—a fine idea is to create a list of top podcasts with either a brief description or a segmented list by topic. Then put your business brand and info on it. I can pretty much guarantee folks will keep that list handy. And your business emblazoned on it means that every time they look at it, they will see your company. I have created a short list of a few that you can use in the Sample appendix, and you'll find others in the Resources section.

Jan 17 Judgement Day—How does your business measure up? Today is a great day to step back and evaluate your successes and failures. Sending surveys to your customers and clients will remind them of your offerings and let them know you value their opinion.

If you have the 2015 edition of the *Weird & Wacky Holiday Marketing Guide,* in it you will find a "Customer Feedback Survey" in its Sample appendix that you can refer to when creating your questions.

Notecards or emails allow you to send a quick note celebrating Judgement Day. Don't worry, all you really need to do it wish others a Happy Judgement Day. Yes, it's just that simple.

Jan 30 National Croissant Day—Recipes are the theme of the day, So, offer up a list of recipes that utilize this tender ingredient. When you create a recipe book, whether you choose print or digital format, you can add your brand to the footnote to keep your business always visible. You'll find a few of my personal favorites in the Samples appendix.

An even easier way to celebrate is to send a card wishing your customers or clients a Happy National Croissant Day. Again, you'll find some quick and easy recipes you can brand and use in your precious recipe book.

Going off on another tangent, since this is a French pastry, why not do something typically French!? Posting photos of yourself, your clients, or even your pets dressed Frenchly on social media could create a stir. Sorry, I couldn't help myself! LOL. Another alternative, along this vein, is to simply post facts about France or famous French chefs. Keep your creative juices flowing this month and I'm sure you'll come up with some additional fun ways to celebrate this weird and wacky holiday.

FEBRUARY

MONTH-LONG HOLIDAYS

Feb 1 – 18 Canada: Winterlude
Feb 9 – Mar 31 Arizona Renaissance Festival (weekends only)

AMD/Low Vision Awareness Month, *American Heart Month, Bake for Family Fun Month, Declutter for a Cause Month, Feline Fix by Five Month, International Boost Self-Esteem Month, Library Lovers Month, Marfan Syndrome Awareness Month, National African-American History Month, National Bird-Feeding Month, National Black History Month, National Cherry Month, National Condom Month, National Mend A Broken Heart Month, National Parent Leadership Month, National Pet Dental Health Month, National Time Management Month, Plant the Seeds of Greatness Month, Return Shopping Carts to the Supermarket Month, Spay/Neuter Awareness Month, Spunky Old Broads Month, Wise Health Care Consumer Month, Worldwide Renaissance of the Heart Month, Youth Leadership Month

WEEK-LONG HOLIDAYS

Feb 3 – 9 African Heritage and Health Week
Feb 7 – 10 Gold Rush Days
Feb 7 – 18 Florida State Fair
Feb 8 – 14 Love Makes the World Go Round; but, Laughter Keeps Us from Getting Dizzy Week
Feb 10 – 16 International Flirting Week
Feb 11 – 15 Freelance Writers Appreciation Week
Feb 11 – 17 Love a Mensch Week
Feb 15 – 18 Great Backyard Bird Count
Feb 15 – 24 National Date Festival (Indio, CA)
Feb 17 – 23 Build a Better Trade Show Image Week, National Engineers Week, Random Acts of Kindness Week
Feb 22 – 23 Texas Cowboy Poetry Gathering

DAILY HOLIDAYS

1. Bubble Gum Day, Car Insurance Day, Freedom Day, G. I. Joe Day, National Candy-Making Day, National Wear Red Day, *Robinson Crusoe Day
2. Bonza Bottler Day™, *Candelmas, *Groundhog Day, *Hedgehog Day, *Imbolic Sled Dog Day, Mexico: Dia de la Candelaria, The Record of a Sneeze Day (125th Anniversary), Take Your Child to the Library Day
3. *Four Chaplains Memorial Day, *The Day, The Music Died Day (60th Anniversary, 1959), *Income Tax Birthday, Japan: Bean Throwing Festival Day (Setsubun), Mozambique: Heroes' Day, Switzerland: Homstom, Vietnam: National Holiday

4. Abraham Lincoln Birthday Celebration, Angola: Armed Struggle Day, *Facebook Launch Day (2004), Lindbergh Day, Medjool Date Day, *Rosa Parks Birthday (1913), Sri Lanka: Independence Day, *USO Day, World Cancer Day
5. Chinese New Year, *Family Leave Bill (1993), Longest War in History Ends (1985), Mexico: Constitution Day, Move Hollywood and Broadway to Lebanon, *Weatherperson's Day, Witherspoon Day
6. Accession of Queen Elizabeth II (1952), National Girls and Women in Sports Day, National Signing Day, New Zealand: Waitangi Day, United Nations: International Day of Zero Tolerance for Female Genital Mutilation
7. *Ballet Day, *Chaplin's "Tramp" Day (1914), *Charles Dickens (1812), Granada: Independence Day, National Black HIV/AIDS Awareness Day, *Wave All Your Fingers at Your Neighbor's Day
8. *Boy Scouts of America Day (1910), Japan: Ha-Ri-Ku-Yo (Needle Mass), Opera Debut in the Colonies Day (1735), Slovenia: Culture Day
9. *Beatles Day (55th Anniversary of appearance on The Ed Sullivan Show, 1964), *Ernest Tubb (1914), *Gypsy Rose Lee (1914), Lebanon: St. Maron's Day, National Pizza Day, Read in a Bathtub Day, Union Officers Escape Libby Prison (1864)
10. *"All the News That's Fit to Print" Day, *Charles Lamb (1775), *First Computer Chess Victory over Human (1996), *First WWII Medal of Honor (1942), Man Day, *Plimsoll Day, Treaty of Paris (1763)
11. Cameroon: Youth Day, *First Woman Episcopal Bishop (1989), Get Out Your Guitar Day, Iran: Victory of Islamic Revolution, *Japan: National Foundation Day, Mandela Released Day (1990), *National Shut-in Visitation Day, *Pro Sports Wives Day, *Satisfied Staying Single Day, *Thomas Alva Edison Birthday (1847), United Nations: International Day of Women and Girls in Science, White Shirt Day
12. *Darwin Day, *Dracula Day, *Abraham Lincoln (1809) and Birthplace Cabin Wreath Laying Day, Myanmar: Union Day, NAACP Day (1909), *Oglethorpe Day, *Safetypup's® Day
13. *Employee Legal Awareness Day, *First Magazine Published (1741), *Get a Different Name Day, Wingman's Day, Self-Love Day, World Radio Day
14. ENIAC Computer Day, *Ferris Wheel Day, *First Presidential Photograph Day (1849), *League of Women Voters Day, National Donor Day, Race Relations Day, *Saint Valentine's Day
15. Afghanistan: Soviet Troop Withdrawal (1989), Asteroid Near Miss Day, Canada: Maple Leaf Flag Day, *Chelyabinsk Meteor Explosion (2013), *Galileo, Galilei (1564), Love Reset Day, *Lupercalia, *Remember the Maine Day, Serbia: National Day, *Susan B. Anthony Day
16. Lithuania: Independence Day, World Pangolin Day
17. Daytona 500, *League of United Latin American Citizens (LULAC) Founded (1929), *My Way Day, *National PTA Founders Day, Random Acts of Kindness Day
18. Canada: Family Day (Selected Provinces), Gambia: Independence Day, Helen Gurley Brown Day, Nepal: National Democracy Day, Presidents' Day, Washington's Birthday Observed, *Pluto (Planet) Day
19. Bollingen Prize Day (Poetry 70th Anniversary, 1949), *Japanese Internment Day, Knights of Pythias Day
20. Ansel Adams Day (1925), Closest Approach of a Comet to Earth (1941), *Northern Hemisphere Hoodie Hoo Day (at high noon everyone yells "HoodiE-Hoo" to chase away winter and make way for spring.), *United Nations: World Day for Social Justice

21. Bangladesh: Martyrs Day, Erma Bombeck Day (1927), CIA Agent Arrested as Spy Day (1994), Introduce a Girl to Engineering Day (Discovere Girl Day), *United Nations: International Mother Language Day, *Washington Monument Dedicated (1885)
22. *George Washington's Birthday (1732), Montgomery Boycott Arrests Day (1956), National Margarita Day, Saint Lucia: Independence Day, Woolworth's Day (1879)
23. Brunei Darussalam: National Day, *Curling is Cool Day, Diesel Engine Day, First Cloning of an Adult Animal (1997), Guyana: Anniversary of Republic, *Iwo Jima Day (flag raised), Open That Bottle Night, Russia: Defender of the Fatherland Day, Single Tasking Day, World Sword Swallower's Day
24. Estonia: Independence Day, Gregorian Calendar Day (1582), Mexico: Flag Day, Steve Jobs Birthday (1955), *Wilhelm Carl Grimm (1786)
25. *Jim Backus Birthday (1913), Kuwait: National Day
26. Buffalo Bill Cody Day (1846), *Federal Communications Commission Created (FCC), (1934), *For Pete's Sake Day, Kuwait: Liberation Day, *Levi Strauss Day, World Spay Day
27. Dominican Republic: Independence Day, *Henry Wadsworth Longfellow Birthday (1807), International Polar Bear Day, Twenty-Second Amendment to US Constitution Ratification (1951)
28. Digital Learning Day, Floral Design Day, National Chili Day, *National Tooth Fairy Day, Taiwan: Peace Memorial Day

HOLIDAY MARKETING IDEAS FOR FEBRUARY

National Mend a Broken Heart Month — Volunteer or organize a drive to support the Foster care system in your local community this month. I have put instructions on organizing a drive in the Sample appendix. Also, you will find there a fact sheet and card you are free to brand and distribute.

If you have been considering becoming a foster parent, I found a list that may help you which I have repeated in the appendix as well.

Feb 1 Freedom Day — Old Abe got it right! Freedom is not to be taken for granted. It can come in many forms, freedom from tyranny, bullying, fear, and even stress are all topics of concern this day. Coaches will find this a perfect opportunity to host a seminar, webinar, or even a Facetime or Google Hangout event.

However, even you can promote your business today. Simple ways to celebrate include sending cards or posting on social media. Check out the images in the Sample appendix that you can freely use. But, be sure to brand it to your business when you do. I have created them with minimal text so you won't get Facebook slapped when you attempt to use them.

Feb 4 Facebook Launch Day — Facebook has certainly evolved over the years. To celebrate their 15th anniversary be sure to use one of their most recent additions, and host, or at least participate in, a FaceTime or Factbook Live event. When you plan this far enough in advance, so you have time to promote your event, you're sure to have a good attendance.

If I may, I would suggest at least one of your speakers should discuss the many features and benefits of using Facebook and its myriad of tools. After all, it is all about Facebook today. And, if you just happen to offer coaching or services in this area, even if you are a Virtual Assistant (VA) you might just end up with a new client or two.

Feb 11 – 17 Love a Mensch Week — I don't know about you, but I didn't have a clue what a mensch was when I saw the name of this weird and wacky holiday. So, I looked it up. It turns out a mensch is a person of integrity who you seek to emulate. There are two sides to this week-long celebration — shower your mensch with acts of gratitude or seek to become someone else's mensch. Either way you go, let your voice be heard and your feelings known.

A more interesting way you can celebrate is by holding a "Love a Mensch" writing contest. Since you have the whole week to use, seek short essays and award the most touching author or author's mensch, or both, a valuable prize appropriate to the winner's essay. If you can find a sponsor who will donate a gift certificate, they may even help you promote your contest. This will expose your business be to a larger audience. Good for you, good for them, and good for your winner(s).

Feb 17 – 23 Random Acts of Kindness Day & Week — Feb 17th is Random Acts of Kindness Day, but it overflows, as your RAKs should, into a week-long celebration. I can think of a plethora of ways to celebrate this weird and wacky holiday, as you probably can too.

The most obvious idea is to create branded RAK cards, then go out into the world and perform a RAK for someone. When you do, hand them a card that basically lets them know that they are a victim of RAK Week. You'll find a sample in the appendix. Furthermore, if you do it on a grand scale—donating to a cause or sponsoring an event—and let the media know your intentions well enough in advance they will, most likely, highlight you and your business on at least one segment.

If you happen to have the 2014 edition of the *Weird & Wacky Holiday Marketing Guide*, you are in luck! Among the appendix samples you will find suggestions on ways you can perform RAKs that is only a brief list culled from RandomActsofKindness.org's list of over 332 kindness ideas.

There's even a bookmark template that you can use to create your own RAK bookmarks, if you would rather create and hand out bookmarks instead of cards, available there.

Feb 27 International Polar Bear Day — To finish off this chilly month we look to the arctic bear. During my foray, I learned that the polar bear is the only bear that is classified as a marine

mammal. Did you know that? I certainly didn't. What other fun facts can you come up with to post on your social media channels?

Cards, fact sheets, donating to a zoo (time or money), and social media graphics are all good ways to celebrate today. If you need help getting started, be sure to check out the samples in the appendix for some ideas you can brand and use or just jump-start your own creativity.

MARCH

MONTH-LONG HOLIDAYS

Mar 2–17 Iditarod Trail Sled Dog Race
Mar 6–Apr 20 Orthodox Lent
Mar 13–Apr 15 Deaf History Month

Alport Syndrome Awareness Month, American Red Cross Month, Colorectal Cancer Awareness Month, Credit Education Month, Employee Spirit Month, Humorists Are Artists Month, International Black Women in Jazz Month, International Ideas Month, International Mirth Month, Irish-American Heritage Month, Music in our Schools Month, National Clean Up Your IRS Act Month, National Colorectal Cancer Awareness Month (Different sponsor from Colorectal Cancer Awareness Month), National Craft Month, National Kidney Month, National Multiple Sclerosis Education and Awareness Month, National Nutrition Month®, National Peanut Month, National Umbrella Month, National Women's History Month, Optimism Month, Paws to Read Month, Play the Recorder Month, Poison Prevention Awareness Month, Red Cross Month, Save the Vaquita Month, Save YoFur Vision Month, Sing with Your Child Month, Social Work Month, Worldwide Home Schooling Awareness Month, Youth Art Month

WEEK-LONG HOLIDAYS

Mar 1–2 National Day of Unplugging
Mar 1–7 National Cheerleading Week, Will Eisner Week
Mar 3–5 Shrovetide
Mar 3–9 Celebrate Your Name Week, National Consumer Protection Week, Return the Borrowed Books Week, Teen Tech Week, Telecommuter Appreciation Week
Mar 4–5 Fasching
Mar 4–8 National School Breakfast Week
Mar 8–15 HeForShe Arts Week
Mar 10–16 Termite Awareness Week
Mar 11–17 Brain Awareness Week, Turkey Vultures Return to the Living Sign
Mar 12–14 London Book Fair
Mar 14–17 Emerald City Comic Con
Mar 14–21 Special Olympics 2019 World Summer Games
Mar 16–17 Military Through the Ages
Mar 17–23 National Poison Prevention Week, World Folk Tales and Fables Week
Mar 18–24 Act Happy Week, International Teach Music Week, United Kingdom: Shakespeare Week Wellderly Week
Mar 21–27 United Nations: Week of Solidarity with the Peoples Struggling Against Racism and Racial Discrimination
Mar 22–24 American Crossword Puzzle Tournament

Mar 24 – 30 National Protocol Officers' Week
Mar 29 – 31 Chicago Comic and Entertainment Expo (C2E2)

DAILY HOLIDAYS

1. Baby Sleep Day, Bosnia and Herzegovina: Independence Day, Dress in Blue Day, *Iceland: Beer Day, Korea: Samiljol or Independence Movement Day, Landmine Ban Day, National Horse Protection Day, *National Pig Day, NEA's Read Across America Day, Paraguay: National Heroes' Day, *Peace Corps Founded (1961), Plan a Solo Vacation Day, *Refired, Not Retired Day, Shabbat Across America and Canada, Switzerland: Chalandrea Maraz, Wales: Saint David's Day, World Day of Prayer Zero Discrimination Day
2. Dr Seuss Day, Ethiopia: Adwa Day, *Highway Numbers Day, *King Kong Premier (1933)
3. Alexander Graham Bell (1847), *Bonza Bottler Day™, Bulgaria: Liberation Day, Fasching Sunday, International Ear Care Day, Japan: Hina Matsuri (Doll Festival), Malawi: Martyr's Day, Namesake Day, *National Anthem Day (1931), Orthodox Meatfare Sunday, Simplify-Your-Life Day, United Nations: World Wildlife Day, *What If Cats and Dogs Had Opposable Thumbs Day, World Birth Defects Day
4. Australia: Eight Hour Day or Labor Day, Fun Facts About Names Day, Guam: Discovery Day or Magellan Day, Iceland: Bun Day, National Backcountry Ski Day, *National Grammar Day, Old Inauguration Day, Old Inauguration Day, Shrove Monday
5. Iceland: Bursting Day, Mardi Gras, National Poutine Day, Paczki Day, Peace Corps Day, Saint Piran's Day, Town Meeting Day, Unique Names Day, Unites States Bank Holiday
6. Ash Wednesday, Discover What Your Name Means Day, *Dred Scott Day, Ghana: Independence Day, *Michelangelo (1475)
7. Nametag Day, United Kingdom and Ireland: World Book Day
8. International Working Women's Day, Middle Name Pride Day, National Proofreading Day, Russia: International Women's Day, Syrian Arab Republic: Revolution Day, United Nations: International Women's Day, United States Income Tax (1913)
9. *Barbie Day, Belize: Baron Bliss Day, Genealogy Day, International Fanny Pack Day, Panic Day, Saint Frances of Rome: Feast Day, Vespucci Day
10. Check Your Batteries Day, Daylight Savings Time Begins, International Bagpipe Day, *Mario Day, National Women and Girls HIV/AIDS Awareness Day, Orthodox Forgiveness Sunday (Cheesefare), *Salvation Army Day, *Telephone Invention Day, *US Paper Money Day
11. Dream 2019 Day, Fill Our Staplers Day (also Nov 4), *Johnny Appleseed Day, Lithuania: Restitution of Independence Day, National Napping Day, Orthodox Green Monday, United Kingdom: Commonwealth Day
12. *FDR's First Fireside Chat (1933), Gabon: National Day, *Girl Scout Day, Great Blizzard Day, Moshoeshoe's Day, Mauritius: Independence Day
13. *Earmuffs Day, Good Samaritan Involvement Day, Holy See: National Day, National Open an Umbrella Indoors Day, Registered Dietitian Nutritionist Day, Smart and Sexy Day
14. *Albert Einstein Birthday (1879), Moth-er Day, Pi Day (as in the math pie = 3.14159265 etc.), "10 Most Wanted List" Day, World Kidney Day
15. Belarus: Constitution Day, Brutus Day, Ides of March, International Day of Action for the Seals, Liberia: JJ Roberts Day, True Confessions Day
16. *Black Press Day (1827), Curlew Day, Freedom of Information Day, Goddard Day, *Lips Appreciation Day, National Panda Day, National Quilting Day, No Selfies Day, Play the Recorder Day, Save the Florida Panther Day

17. *Campfire USA Day, Evacuation Day, Ireland: National Day, Saint Patrick's Day
18. Aruba: Flag Day, Australia: Canberra Day, Diesel Day, Forgive Mom and Dad Day, *National Biodiesel Day
19. Iran: National Day of Oil, National Agriculture Day, Saint Joseph's Day, Swallows Return to San Juan Capistrano Day, US Standard Time Act (100th Anniversary), *Wyatt Earp (1848)
20. *Great American Meat Out Day, Ostara, *Proposal Day®, Ta'anit Esther, Snowman Burning, Tunisia: Independence Day, United Nations: French Language Day, *United Nations: International Day of Happiness, *Won't You Be My Neighbor Day
21. Absolutely Incredible Kid Day, *Bach Day, *First Round-the-World Balloon Flight (20th Anniversary, 1999),India: Holi, Iranian New Year: (Noruz), Japan: Vernal Equinox Day, Lesotho: National Tree Planting Day, Memory Day, Namibia: Independence Day, National Healthy Fats Day, Naw-Ruz, Purim, South Africa: Human Rights Day, *Twitter Day, *United Nations: International Day for the Elimination of Racial Discrimination, United Nations: International Day of Forests, United Nations: International Nowruz Day, United Nations: World Poetry Day, World Down Syndrome Day
22. As Young As You Feel Day, India: New Year's Day, *International Day of The Seal, *Louis L'Amour Day (1908), Laser Patented Day (1960), *National Goof-off Day, Puerto Rico: Emancipation Day, United Nations: World Day for Water (aka World Water Day)
23. Beat the Clock Day, "Big Bertha Paris Gun Day, *Liberty Day, National Puppy Day, National Tamale Day, *Near Miss Day, "OK" Day, Pakistan: Republic Day, *United Nations: World Meteorological Day
24. Argentina: National Day of Memory for Truth and Justice, Exxon Valdez Oil Spill (1989), *Houdini Day (1874), Philippine Independence, United Nations: International Day for the Right to the Truth Concerning Gross Human Rights Violations and for the Dignity of Victims, *World Tuberculosis Day
25. *Bed In for Peace Day, *Greece: Independence Day: National Day of Celebration of Greek and American Democracy, Maryland Day, National Medal of Honor Day, *Old New Year's Day, Pecan Day, Seward's Day, Tolkien Reading Day, United Nations: International Day of Remembrance of The Victims of Slavery and The Transatlantic, United Nations: International Day of Solidarity with Detained and Missing Staff Members
26. American Diabetes Association Alert Day, Education and Sharing Day, Bangladesh: Independence Day, Camp David Accord Day, *Legal Assistants Day, Live Long and Prosper Day, *Make Up Your Own Holiday Day
27. Alaska: Earthquake (55th Anniversary, 1964), *FDA Approves Viagra Day, Little Red Wagon Day, Manatee Appreciation Day, *Quirky Country Music Song Titles Day, Whole Grain Sampling Day
28. Big Bang Day, Czech Republic: Teachers' Day
29. *Canada: British North America Act (1867), Central African Republic: Boganda Day, Dow Jones Day, *Knights of Columbus Founders Day, *Niagara Falls Runs Dry (1848), Taiwan: Youth Day
30. Anesthetic Day, *Doctors Day, Earth Hour, Grass is Always Browner on the Other Side of the Fence Day, International Laundry Folding Day, *Pencil Day, Trinidad and Tobago: Spiritual/Shouter Baptist Liberation Day, Vincent Van Gogh Day (1853), World Bipolar Day
31. *Bunsen Burner Day, Cesar Chavez Day, *Eiffel Tower Day (1998), England: Mothering Sunday, European Union: Daylight Savings Time (Summertime begins), International Hug a Medievalist Day, Luxembourg: Bretzeldsonndeg, *National "She's Funny That Way" Day, World Back-up Day

HOLIDAY MARKETING IDEAS FOR MARCH

International Mirth Month — I can't imagine not focusing on this weird and wacky holiday in the *Weird & Wacky Holiday Marketing Guide!* This month's focus is on putting more fun in your business marketing, for sure. Nevertheless, don't fail to see the humor in even the most mundane situations.

The whole month you can offer tips, if not daily, at least weekly on how to change your point of view on different situations. Close each tidbit with a bit of humor if you can.

If you don't think you can do this by yourself, you could ask a coach or speaker to share their expertise. However, try not to give too much 'expertise' away to others. You are trying, after all, to build your fan base and not theirs!

Mar 1 Baby Sleep Day — Every year, while preparing this book, I read about all kinds of weird and wacky holidays that focus on this or that disease. But, when I read about Baby Sleep Day, this year being named for the first time ever, I realized just how integral being well rested is to our overall health.

The question is, how do we turn this weird and wacky holiday into a marketing opportunity? Beauty, bath, aroma therapy, stress coaches, VA's … all kinds of businesses could benefit from sharing the benefits of rest and relaxation. Even bars and restaurants!

From tips and techniques shared in the form of social media posts, seminars, webinars, Facetime chats, Google hangouts, emails, and even cards you'll soon discover a ton of opportunities to tie this restful holiday into your marketing plan for March.

Mar 4 Fun Facts About Names Day — What's in a name? Isn't that the question Shakespeare pondered in his infamous play, *Romeo and Julet*? Why not take the time to look up not only your own name, but your best, most loyal customer names too? With just a tiny bit of research you could come up with enough information to make a nice card or calligraphy to send to them that, of course, you have branded to your business. As you can see this can be done easily.

This is one piece they will want to keep, and who knows, they may even frame it! Talk about marketing success! You'll have them thinking of you every time they look at it. And I would bet they would proudly show it to their friends. I'm just sayin' ….

If you don't do calligraphy, a quick Google search will turn up several who may be willing to assist you. Also, you will find a Facebook and Twitter graphic you can customize and use for your social media postings.

Mar 13 Smart and Sexy Day — This weird and wacky holiday was created to give women the confidence and knowledge they need to succeed in the workforce. Begin by offering seminars, workshops, personal image classes, employment interview training, resume writing tips and techniques, and general advice.

While all of these done online or locally would help solidify your expertise by just sponsoring, planning, or hosting an event like these, imagine how much media attention you could possibly get when you offer these training sessions for free to women and girls of lower to middle income who would otherwise never get this kind of help. You could change a life, and that life could be yours!

Mar 24 Twitter Day — Last month we celebrated everything Facebook has to offer. Today, our focus is on Twitter. Tweet your heart out! Share your events and advice, tips, articles, and images. Keep on tweeting with those all-important hash tags until the day draws to a close. The more you share the greater your footprint. The greater your footprint, the wider your audience will grow.

When you use HootSuite® or some other tool, your tweet day just got soooo much easier! In the appendix you will find a list of Twitter tools and tips to help you along the way.

Mar 30 International Laundry Folding Day — What does business have to do with laundry folding? Organization! So, to celebrate this definitely weird and wacky holiday organization should be your primary focus.

Start out with topic ideas like, organize your life, your closet, your time, your goals, etc., you get the picture. Then, decide if you are up to organizing a group activity or you need to spend some solo-time working on your own life or business.

You always could opt for the easy way out and just send social media organizational tips out to your social media followers.

#

Apr 7 – 20 Passiontide

MONTH-LONG HOLIDAYS

Adopt a Ferret Month, Alcohol Awareness Month, Black Women's History Month, Community Spirit Days, Couple Appreciation Month, Distracted Driving Awareness Month, Grange Month, Holy Humor Month, Informed Women Month, International Customer Loyalty Month, International Twit Award Month, Jazz Appreciation Month, Library Snapshot Days, Mathematics Awareness Month, National African-American Women's Fitness Month, National Autism Awareness Month, National Cancer Control Month, National Card and Letter Writing Month, National Child Abuse Prevention Month, National Donate Life Month, National Humor Month, National Knuckles Down Month, National Lawn Care Month, National Occupational Therapy Month, National Pecan Month, National Pest Management Month, National Poetry Month, National Rebuilding Month, National Sexual Assault Awareness Month, Nationally Sexually Transmitted Diseases (STDs) Month, National Soy Foods Month, National Youth Sports Safety Month, Pet First Aid Awareness Month, Pharmacists War on Diabetes Month, Prevention of Animal Cruelty Month, Rosacea Awareness Month, School Library Month, Straw Hat Month, Stress Awareness Month, Women's Eye Health and Safety Month, World Landscape Architecture Month, Worldwide Bereaved Spouses Awareness Month

WEEK-LONG HOLIDAYS

Apr 1 – 7 Laugh at Work Week, Orthodox Holy Week, Testicular Cancer Awareness Week (aka Get a Grip Day)
Apr 1 – 4 Italy: Bologna Children's Book Fair
Apr 1 – 6 Explore Your Career Options Week
Apr 4 – 10 Hate Week — "Down with Big Brother"
Apr 8 – 12 National Dental Hygienists Week, Undergraduate Research Week
Apr 7 – 13 National Crime Victims' Rights Week, National Library Week, National Volunteer Week, Passion Week
Apr 11 – 14 French Quarter Festival
Apr 14 – 20 Greece: Dumb Week, Holy Week, National Dog Bite Prevention Week, Pan-American Week, Philippines: Holy Week
April 20 – 27 Pesach or Passover
Apr 20 – 28 National Park Week (tentative)
Apr 21 – 27 Administrative Professionals Week, Chemists Celebrate Earth Week, Orthodox Holy Week, Preservation Week, Sky Awareness Week
Apr 24 – 30 World Immunization Week
Apr 25 – 28 Fiddler's Frolics
Apr 27 – 28 Just Pray No! Worldwide Weekend of Prayer and Fasting

Apr 28 – May 4 Small Business Week
Apr 29 – May 5 Japan: Golden Week Days

DAILY HOLIDAYS

1. *April Fool's or All Fool's Day, Bulgaria: St Lasarus' Day, Canada: Nunavut Independence (20th Anniversary, 1999), Iran: Islamic Republic Day, Mule Day, Mylesday, *Sorry Charlie Day, US Air Force Academy Day
2. Argentina: Malvinas Day, Hans Christian Anderson Day (1805), *International Children's Book Day, *Sir Alec Guinness (1914), Love Your Produce Manager Day, National Ferret Day, Ponce de Leon Discovers Florida (1513), *Reconciliation Day, *United Nations: World Autism Awareness Day, US Mint Day
3. Blacks Ruled Eligible to Vote Day (1944), *Pony Express Day, National Weed Out Hate: Sow the Seeds of Peace Day, *Tweed Day
4. Angelou, Maya Birthday (1928), *Beatles Take Over Music Charts (1964), *Bonza Bottler Day™, Flag Act of 1818 Day, Senegal: Independence Day, Taiwan: Children's Day, *United Nations: International Day for Mine Awareness and Assistance in Mine Action, *Vitamin C Day
5. Gold Star Spouses Day, International Kids Yoga Day, National Deep Dish Pizza Day
6. Drowsy Driver Awareness Day, International Pillow Fight Day, National Love Your Children Day, North Pole Discovery Day, *Tartan Day, *Teflon Day (1938), Thailand: Chakri Day, United Nations: International Day of Sport for Development and Peace
7. *International Beaver Day, International Snailpapers Day, *Metric System Day, National Beer Day (1933), National Making the First Move Day, *No Housework Day, United Nations: International Day of the Reflection on the Genocide in Rwanda, *United Nations: World Health Day
8. Home Run Record Set by Hank Aaron (1974), International Roma Day, Japan: Flower Festival (Hana Matsuri), National Dog Fighting Awareness Day
9. Children's Day in Florida (always the second Tuesday), *Civil Rights Bill of 1866 Day, Civil War Ends (1865), International Be Kind to Lawyers Day, *Jenkins Ear Day, Jumbo the Elephant Day, National Former Prisoner of War Recognition Day, National Library Workers Day, Philippines: Araw Ng Kagitingan, Texas Panhandle Tornado Day, Tunisia: Martyrs' Day, *Winston Churchill Day
10. ASPCA Incorporation Day (1866), *Commodore Perry Day, National Bookmobile Day, *National Siblings Day, *Salvation Army Founder's Day
11. *Barbershop Quartet Day, Civil Rights Act Day (1968), *International "Louie Louie" Day, National Pet Day, World Parkinson's Day
12. Halifax: Independence Day, *National D.E.A.R. Day (aka Drop Everything and Read), *National Licorice Day, National Teach Children to Save Day, Polio Vaccine Day, Truancy Day, United Nations: International Day of Human Space Flight, *Walk on Your Wild Side Day, Yuri's Night
13. *Guy Fawkes Day, Sri Lanka: Sinhala and Tamil New Year, *Thomas Jefferson Day
14. *Children with Alopecia Day, Dictionary Day, India: Vaisakhi, *International Moment of Laughter Day, Palm Sunday, Pan-American Day, Pathologists' Assistant Day
15. Astronomers Find New Solar System (20th Anniversary, 1999), 123rd Boston Marathon and Bombing (2013), Botox Day, *McDonald's Day, *Income Tax Pay Day, *National Take a Wild

Guess Day, *National That Sucks Day, Quarterly Estimated Federal Income Tax Payers' Due Date (also Jan 15, Jun 17, and Sep 16, 2018), *Titanic Sinking (1912)
16. *Charlie Chaplin Day (1889), Education and Sharing Day, Emancipation Day, National Stress Awareness Day
17. American Samoa: Flag Day, *Blah! Blah! Blah! Day, Herbalist Day, International Haiku Poetry Day, Syrian Arab Republic: Independence Day
18. Canada: Constitution Act of 1982, Get to Know Your Customers Day (third Thursday of each quarter is set aside to get to know your customers even better), The House that Ruth Built Day, *International Amateur Radio Day, Maundy Thursday or Holy Thursday, National High Five Day, Paul Revere's Ride Day (1775), *Pet Owners Independence Day, "Third World" Day, World Heritage Day/International Day for Monuments and Sites, Zimbabwe: Independence Day
19. Good Friday, John Parker Day, National Hanging Out Day, Passover (begins at sundown), Patriots Day in Florida, Swaziland: King's Birthday
20. Easter Even, International Raw Milk Cheese Appreciation Day, Lazarus Saturday, United Nations: Chinese Language Day
21. Aggie Muster Day, Brazil: Tiradentes Day, Easter Sunday, Indonesia: Kartini Day, Italy: Birthday of Rome, *Kindergarten Day, National Bulldogs are Beautiful Day, Orthodox Palm Sunday, San Jacinto Day
22. Brazil Day, Coins Stamped "In God We Trust" Day, *Confederate Memorial Day, Dyngus Day USA, *Earth Day, Easter Monday, *National Jelly Bean Day, Oklahoma Land Rush Day (1889), South Africa: Family Day, United Nations: International Mother Earth Day
23. Canada: Newfoundland: Saint George's Day, *Movie Theatre Day, *Public School Day, National English Muffin Day, Saint George Feast Day, Spain: Book Day and Lover's Day, Turkey: National Sovereignty and Children's Day, William Shakespeare Day (1564), Spain: Book Day and Lover's Day, Turkey: National Sovereignty and Children's Day, United Nations: English Language Day, United Nations: Spanish Language Day, *United Nations: World Book and Copyright Day, World Book Night
24. Administrative Professionals Day or Secretary's Day, Armenia: Armenian Martyrs Day, Ireland: Easter Rising (1916), Library of Congress Day
25. Abortion Legalized (1967), Anzac Day, Egypt: Sinai Day, *License Plates Day, Italy: Liberation Day, Portugal: Liberty Day, Swaziland: National Flag Day, Take Our Daughters and Sons to Work® Day (fourth Thursday in April), World Malaria Day, World Penguin Day, East Meets West Day
26. Audubon Day, Florida and Georgia: Confederate Memorial Day, *Hug an Australian Day, National Arbor Day, National Hairball Awareness Day, National Help a Horse Day, National Pretzel Day, *Richter Scale Day, Tanzania: Union Day, United Nations: International Chernobyl Disaster Remembrance Day, United Nations: World Intellectual Property Day
27. *Babe Ruth Day (1947), Independent Bookstore Day, Mantanzas Mule Day, *Morse Code Day, Most Tornadoes in a Day (US), National Dance Day, National Little Pampered Dog Day, National Rebuilding Day, Netherlands: King's Day, Record Store Day, Sierra Leon and Togo: Independence Day, Slovenia: Insurrection Day, South Africa, Freedom Day, World Healing Day, World Tai Chi and Qigong Day, World Veterinary Day
28. Biological Clock Gene Discovered (1994), Canada: National Day of Mourning, Orthodox Easter Sunday or Pascha, Switzerland: Landsgemeinde, United Nations: World Day for Safety and Health at Work, Workers Memorial Day
29. Japan: Showa Day, *"Peace" Rose Day, Zipper Day (1913)

30. Beltane, *Bugs Bunny Day (1938), Día de los Niños/Día de los Libros, International Jazz Day, National Animal Advocacy Day, National Honesty Day (Honest Abe Awards), Raisin Day, Vietnam: Liberation Day, *Walpurgis Night

HOLIDAY MARKETING IDEAS FOR APRIL

Holy Humor Month—Good clean fun is to be celebrated this month. If laughter is said to be good medicine, then religious joy and humor is a celebration of the soul! So, this month share the mirth at every opportunity, but keep it on the upside of humor.

If you don't know any good clean jokes, ask your pastor, or check out a few I have gleaned over time in the appendix.

Apr 2 International Children's Book Day—Spend the day inspiring a love for reading in the younger generation. Consider time spent at a library or pre-school reading stories to the little ones or donate books if you have more money than time. Libraries are always in need of donations. And, if you are a children's book author the task of finding appropriate books for children and young adults just got easier. If you coordinate with other authors in your area to donate your time or books, be sure to let the media in on your intentions.

At the very least you could put a notice in your local paper honoring this weird and wacky holiday. If you decide to opt for an advertisement, you'll find a sample in the appendix that you can customize and use.

April 7 National Beer Day—Does that mean that April 6 is New Beer's Eve? While researching this weird and wacky holiday I discovered that there are four types of beer; stout and porters, lagers, malts, and ales and a whole lot of styles. There are not just the familiar amber and dark, but others called blondes, cream, brown, fruit, golden, honey. Is that enough choice for you? If not, there's also Indian pale ale, of course light, lime, pale, pilsner, red, strong, and wheat! And that's just the beginning. One website touts 75+ varieties! No wonder we have National Beer Day.

To celebrate have a sip of your favorite or discover a new favorite. Have a celebration and invite your beer loving clients to join you, or perhaps in a virtual libation is in order. But, remember to imbibe responsibly.

Another way to enjoy this holiday while keeping your marketing in mind is to share a few well-timed factoids on your social media, or tweet with the hashtag #nationalbeerday or just simply #beer to keep the conversation going. While you are thinking about it, you might even consider having a brewing friend explain the intricacies of the brewing process to a group of soon-to-be home brewers either online or at a live event. This could make for an interesting party if you make it hands-on.

Oh, and there's always the tried and true social media graphics you can post or even create a video to share. If you need a spark for your design imagination check out the Samples appendix.

Apr 12 Truancy Day — This weird and wacky holiday speaks to the problems with misspent youth. But truancy is a problem even for adults, especially those of us who are in business for ourselves. Yes, even I have trouble staying on task — sometimes. So, to divest yourself of your nefarious ways, ofttimes it's best to seek the advice of a professional. And, since you aren't alone, why not host an event that helps others hear from you and others that may give them ideas how to overcome their wayward ways? When you host or sponsor an event it can give your business the leg up over your competition who have let this marketing opportunity slip away.

Again, tweeting and posting on social media is the easy way out. However, if you send out card, yes real physical cards to your customers and clients they will get noticed far more than an email ever could. So, consider sending at least your most loyal customers and clients a note letting them know you are not being truant in letting them know how important they are on this fun day.

Apr 15 Botox Day — In thinking about how to use this day to market a business I am reminded of the effects of Botox and what can happen if you overdo it. Since Botox inflates things that is a good jumping in point for ideas on how to celebrate today. On the negative we have inflated egos and the problems that can cause when you are trying to run a business. So, personal training might be a good focal point.

Then on the positive side, Botox can make you feel better about yourself, and there is your second focus; giving others a boost by teaching them how to build their self-esteem. Whether that means learning how to be better communicators or how to dress properly for business or even interviews, there are numerous subjects and businesses that could really make a go of adding a bit of Botox to their marketing plan. So, webinars, seminars, Google Hangouts, Facebook Live, all are superb tools to boost your business today.

Apr 25 World Penguin Day — Did you know that there are 17 species of penguins, and all their natural habitats are in the Southern hemisphere or that they are birds? Not just any bird, but one in their species is actually the largest of all birds; the Emperor Penguin. You'll find this fact and a few others on the fun facts sheet in the Samples appendix.

Be sure you wear black and white today—penguin colors. However, wearing a tuxedo in their honor is optional. It is also popular today to tell a penguin joke or two or learn a bit about this unique bird.

Another way to celebrate is to make a donation to a charity in honor of penguins. There are many charities that you can donation to, and the money can go towards penguins. Some agencies even allow you to 'adopt' a penguin in your name for charity. If you raise funds for one of these charities and let the media know you might even get some publicity around your generous gift. Oh, and for sure you'll want to use #WorldPenguinDay to share on social media.

MONTH-LONG HOLIDAYS

May 6 – Jun 3 Ramadan: The Islamic Month of Fasting
May 15 – 26 Cannes Film Festival
May 30 – Jul 14 Cricket World Cup

Asian/Pacific American Heritage Month, Asthma Awareness Month, Better Hearing and Speech Month, Fibromyalgia Education and Awareness Month, Gardening for Wildlife Month, Get Caught Reading Month, Gifts from the Garden Month, Global Civility Awareness Month, Haitian Heritage Month, Heal the Children Month, Huntington's Disease Awareness Month, International Mediterranean Diet Month, International Victorious Woman Month, Jewish American Heritage Month, Law Enforcement Appreciation Month in Florida, Mental Health Month, Motorcycle Safety Month, Mystery Month, National Allergy/Asthma Awareness Month, National Arthritis Awareness Month, National Barbecue Month, National Better Hearing Month, National Bike Month, National Foster Care Month, National Good Car-Keeping Month, National Hamburger Month, National Hepatitis Awareness Month, National Meditation Month, National Military Appreciation Month, National Osteoporosis Awareness and Prevention Month, National Preservation Month, National Salad Month, National Stroke Awareness Month, National Sweet Vidalia® Onion Month, National Vinegar Month, Older American's Month, Philippines: Santacruzan, React Month, Skin Cancer Awareness Month, Spiritual Literacy Month, Strike Out Strokes Month, Ultraviolet Awareness Month, Women's Health Care Month, Young Achievers/Leaders of Tomorrow Month

WEEK-LONG HOLIDAYS

May 1 – 7 Choose Privacy Week
May 5 – 11 Be Kind to Animals Week®, National Family Week, National Hug Holiday Week, National Hurricane Preparedness Week, National Pet Week, Root Canal Awareness Week, Update Your References Week
May 6 – 10 PTA Teacher Appreciation Week
May 6 – 12 National Nurses Week
May 12 – 18 National Police Week, National Transportation Week
May 13 – 17 National Etiquette Week
May 13 – 19 National Stuttering Awareness Week
May 12 – 18 Salute to 35+ Moms Week, Work at Home Moms Week
May 16 – 21 National Foul Ball Week
May 17 – 18 Fishing Has No Boundaries Days
May 18 – 24 National Safe Boating Week
May 19 – 25 International New Friends Old Friends Week, National Unicycle Week, World Trade Week

May 23 – 26 Memory Days
May 20 – 27 National Backyard Games Week
May 23 – 26 Monaco: Grand Prix de Monaco (tentative)
May 24 – 26 National Polka Festival
May 26 – Jun 2 National African Violet Week

DAILY HOLIDAYS

1. *Amtrak, Batman Day, Batman Debut Anniversary (1939), Great Britain Formed Day (1707), Hug Your Cat Day, Skyscraper Day, *Keep Kids Alive — Drive 25® Day, Labor Day, *Law Day, *Lei Day, *Loyalty Day, *May Day, May One Day, Mother Goose Day, National Bubba Day, *New Home Owners Day, Russia: International Labor Day, *School Principals' Day
2. Israel: Yom Hashoah, King James Bible Published Day, National Day of Prayer, National Day of Reason, United Nations: World Tuna Day, Red Baron Day
3. Dow Jones Tops 11,000 Day (1999), *Garden Meditation Day, Japan: Constitution Memorial Day, *Lumpy Rug Day, Mexico: Day of the Holy Cross, National Public Radio Day, National Specially-Abled Pets Day, *National Two Different Colored Shoes Day, Poland: Constitution Day (Swieto Trzeciego Maja), *United Nations: World Press Freedom Day
4. China: Youth Day, Curaçao: Memorial Day, Jamaica Discover Day (1494), Free Comic Book Day, *International Respect for Chickens Day, Japan: Greenery Day, Kentucky Derby, Learn to Ride a Bike Day, National Auctioneers Day, National Fitness Day, *Star Wars Day
5. AMA Founded Day (1847), *Bonza Bottler Day™, *Cartoonists Day, *Cinco de Mayo, Ethiopia: Patriots Victory Day, International Day of the Midwife, Japan and South Korea: Children's Day, Motorcycle Mass and Blessing of the Bikes, National Infertility Survival® Day, Netherlands: Liberation Day
6. International Management Accounting Day, *Joseph Brackett Day, Melanoma Monday, *No Diet Day, *No Homework Day, United Kingdom: May Day, Orson Wells Day (1915)
7. Beaufort Scale Day, Cystinosis Awareness Day, Dow Jones Tops 15000 (2013), National Teacher Day, World Asthma Day
8. Czech Republic: Liberation Day, Donate A Day's Wages to Charity Day, England: Heston Furry dance/Flora Day, France: Victory Day, Israel: Remembrance Day (Yom Ha'zikkaron), National Bike to School Day, National Nightshift/Thirdshift Workers Day, National Receptionists Day, National School Nurse Day *No Socks Day, Slovakia: Liberation Day, *United Nations: Time of Remembrance and Reconciliation WWII (8 – 9), *V E Day, *World Red Cross Red Crescent Day
9. European Union Founded (1950), Israel: Independence Day (Yom Ha'atzma'ut), Russia: Victory Day, Uzbekistan: Day or Memory and Honor
10. Fintastic Friday: Giving Sharks a Voice, Golden Spike Driving Day (150th Anniversary (1758), Military Spouse Appreciation Day, World Lupus Day
11. *Eat What You Want Day, International Migratory Bird Day, Italy: Giro D'Italia, Jamestown Day, Letter Carriers' "Stamp Out Hunger" Food Drive, National Babysitters Day, Netherlands: National Windmill Day, Spring Astronomy Day, Stay Up All Night Night, United Nations: World Migratory Bird Day, World Fair Trade Day
12. China & Taiwan: Birthday of Lord Buddha, Florence Nightingale Day, *Limerick Day, Native American Rights Day (1879), Mother's Day, Mother's Day at the Wall, Native American Rights Recognized Anniversary (1879), *Odometer Day,

13. Children of Fallen Patriots Day, National Hummus Day
14. Fahrenheit Day, *Lewis and Clark Expedition Sets Out Day (1804), Smallpox Vaccine Discovery (1796), *The Stars and Stripes Forever Day, *Underground America Day, WAAC Day (1942)
15. Flight Attendant Day, Japan: Aoi Matsuri (Hollyhock Festival), Mexico: San Isidro Day, Nakba Day, National Sliders Day, *Nylon Stockings Day, Paraguay: Independence Day, *Peace Officer Memorial Day, *United Nations: International Day of Families
16. *Academy Awards Day (1929), *Biographer's Day, *First Woman to Climb Mt Everest Day (1975)
17. Endangered Species Day, *First Kentucky Derby Day (1875), International Virtual Assistants Day, *Same-Sex Marriages Day (2004), National Bike to Work Day, National Defense Transportation Day, National Pizza Party Day, Teacher's Day in Florida, *United Nations: World Telecommunications and Information Society Day
18. Armed Forces Day, Birthday of Buddha (Day of Vesak), Fishing Has No Boundaries Day, Haiti: Flag and University Day, *International Museum Day, National Learn to Swim Day, Preakness Stakes, Uruguay: Battle of Las Piedras Day, *Visit Your Relatives Day
19. Bay to Breakers Race Day, *Boys Club Day, Dark Day in New England, Hepatitis Testing Day, Ride a Unicycle Day, Turkey: Youth and Sports Day
20. *Amelia Earhart Atlantic Crossing Day (1932), Cameroon: National Holiday, Canada: Victoria Day, East Timor: Anniversary of Independence, *Eliza Doolittle Day, Lindbergh Flight (1927), Mecklenburg Day, Supply Chain Professionals Day, Neighbor Day, *Weights and Measures Day
21. *American Red Cross Founder's Day, *I Need a Patch for That Day, *National Wait Staff Day, *United Nations: World Day for Cultural Diversity for Dialogue and Development
22. *Canadian Immigrants' Day, Mr. Rogers Neighborhood Day, *National Maritime Day, Sri Lanka: National Heroes Day, *United Nations: International Day for Biological Diversity, US Colored Troops Founders Day, World Goth Day, Yemen: National Day
23. *Bonnie and Clyde Death (1934), *International World Turtle Day®, Lag B'Omer, Morocco: National Day, National Eat More Fruits and Vegetables Day, New York Public Library Day, Sweden: Linnaeus Day, United Nations: International day to End Obstetric Fistula
24. Baseball Under Lights Day, Belize: Commonwealth Day, Brooklyn Bridge Open (1883), *Brother's Day, Declaration of the Bab, Eritrea: Independence Day, International Tiara Day, *Morse Code Day,
25. African Freedom Day, Argentina: Revolution Day, *Greatest Day in Track and Field: Jessie Owens' Day, *Ralph Waldo Emerson Birthday (1803), Jordan: Independence Day, *National Missing Children's Day, *National Tap Dance Day, Poetry Day in Florida, *Towel Day, United Nations: Week of Solidarity with Peoples of Non-Self-Governing Territories
26. Australia: Sorry Day, Georgia: Independence Day, Haiti: Mother's Day, Indianapolis 500-Mile Race, John Wayne (1907), Rogation Sunday, Rural Life or Soil Stewardship Sunday, World Lindy Hop Day
27. *Cellophane Tape Day, First Flight into the Stratosphere (1931), First Running of the Preakness, *Golden Gate Bridge Day, Memorial Day, Prayer for Peace Memorial Day, Switzerland: Pacing the Bounds
28. *Amnesty International Founded (1961), Azerbaijan: Day of the Republic, Ethiopia and Nepal: National Day, *Sierra Club Day, *Slugs Return from Capistrano Day

29. *Amnesty for Southern Rebels Day, Ascension of Baha'u'llah, *Mount Everest Summit Reached (1953), National Senior Health and Fitness Day, *United Nations: International Day of United Nations Peacekeepers, World Otter Day
30. Ascension Day, *First American Daily Newspaper Published (1783), *Indianapolis 500 Anniversary (1911), *Loomis Day, Memorial Day (Traditional), Saint Joan of Arc Feast Day
31. *Copyright Law Passed (1970), *United Nations: World No–Tobacco Day, *Walt Whitman Day, *What You Think Upon Grows Day

HOLIDAY MARKETING IDEAS FOR MAY

International Mediterranean Diet Month — It's time to begin a healthier lifestyle. I have read that those who reside in this region live longer, healthier lives. Who among us don't want those benefits? As we strive toward those goals every health-oriented business and career professional can certainly benefit from focusing on International Mediterranean Diet Month.

Mediterranean Diet

Besides those immediate marketing ideas for the health-conscious you could also focus on feeling better. Exercise, nutrition, and health lead to less stress, and stress-related injuries. So, there you now have coaches and career counselors who can be included as business owners who might benefit from marketing this month's weird and wacky holiday. Now we have aroma and massage therapists, candle sellers, and even make-up representatives who could be added to the mix.

For the rest of us, we can offer tips or seminars, webinars, and the like might also work when your guest speakers are any of the above professionals. Another fine idea would be to host a recipe swap! These can be both fun and entertaining besides which, they can be done as live or virtual events.

May 5 Bonza Bottler Day™ — By now you know what this holiday represents. It's basically a make up your own holiday, holiday. If you can think it, you can make it so. Throw a party, perhaps for no other reason than to throw a party. When you do, invite your clients and customers to join you and enjoy a bit of camaraderie. Get to know them better, ask them how you could improve your business model or what alternative solutions they would suggest that you might consider adding to your business tool kit. Then work to fill those needs in the coming days, months, and years.

May 11 National Babysitters Day — Thank God for babysitters; they keep parents sane! Consider nursery workers, pre-school teachers, after-school programs, and others who take care of our little ones while we busy ourselves with life and work. Let yours know how much they are appreciated today with a word of thanks and a gift they don't expect.

For a way to market your business you might put together a National Babysitters Day emergency contact form, with your brand of course, to hand out to mom- and pop-preneurs. This is something they can place on their refrigerator, and when they do, your business will be seen multiple times throughout the day. When they have a need for your products or services they'll know right where to look. I have created one you can use toward these purposes which you will find in the Samples appendix. Also, in the Resources you will find a link to the Family Emergency Plan form which can be downloaded and filled in digitally and then photos added after printing.

May 16 First Woman to Climb Mt Everest Day—Anshu Jamsenpa was the first woman to climb Mount Everest, and she did it not once, but twice in five days! In 2017 she broke a world record and made global headlines when she became the first woman to conquer the 29,028-feet-tall (8,848 meter) Himalayan giant twice in five days— first on May 16, and then again on May 21 That says a lot about her and women in general. We are strong, we are resilient, we are woman!

So today is a day to celebrate our strengths. Gather your fans and celebrate with motivational and instructional speakers. When you host, or sponsor an event, consider inviting not only those who can afford the ticket, but donate a few comp tickets to those who need a leg up. That's what all the shows I have ever been a part of on the big stage have done, and you should too.

If you let the media know what you are up to, they are sure to support your effort. And when they do, you may just end up getting noticed by your next best client or customer!

May 20 Supply Chain Professionals Day—Did you know that there is a course you can take to become a supply chain professional? It's called Supply Chain Management certificate. Michigan State University offers an eight-week course. There are even a dozen or so supporting organizations, like the CSCMP (Counsel of Supply Chain Management Professionals) and the COPS (Chartered Institute of Procurement & Supply). Who knew? Well, it is a big job and somebody has to do it, right? So, we really should be grateful for their willingness to serve the masses, yes, and even us.

Today is a day to post pictures and celebrate what you do every day— funny memes, photos of your colleagues in action, shout outs and just about anything that you can think of.

Just be sure to use the hashtags #SupplyChainProfessionalsDay and #CSCMP with your social media posts! CSCMP will be participating, liking and sharing your posts and celebrating Supply Chain Professionals all over the world! After all, you too are a business-to-business professional, aren't you? If you aren't you certainly should be.

This is the inaugural 2018 Annual Supply Chain Professionals Day so why not join CSCMP in celebrating today's supply chain management professionals on the inaugural Annual Supply Chain Professionals Day?

One way to celebrate is to use the graphic I have provided in the Samples appendix and put your photo or logo on it, then share it on social media.

JUNE

MONTH-LONG HOLIDAYS

Jun 14 – Jul 7 Copa American

Adopt A Shelter Cat Month, African-American Music Appreciation Month, Audiobook Appreciation Month, Cancer From the Sun Month, Caribbean-American Heritage Month, Cataract Awareness Month, Child Vision Awareness Month, Dementia Care Professionals Month, Effective Communications Month, Entrepreneurs and Do It Yourself Marketing Month, Fireworks Safety Month, Gay and Lesbian Pride Month, Great Outdoors Month, International Men's Month, International Surf Music Month, June Dairy Month, Men's Health Education and Awareness Month, Migraine Awareness Month, National Aphasia Awareness Month, National Bathroom Reading Month, National Candy Month, National Caribbean-American Heritage Month, National GLBT Book Month, National Iced Tea Month, National Oceans Month, National Pollinator Month, National Rivers Month, National Rose Month, Nation Safety Month, National Soul Food Month, National Zoo and Aquarium Month, Perennial Gardening Month, Pharmacists Declare War on Alcoholism Month, PTSD Awareness Month, Rebuild Your Life Month, Skyscraper Month, Student Safety Month

WEEK-LONG HOLIDAYS

Jun 1 – 8 International Clothesline Week
Jun 2 – 8 Bed Bug Awareness Week, National Business Etiquette Week
Jun 9 – 10 Shavuot or Feast of Weeks
Jun 9 – 15 Greencare for Troops Awareness Week, National Flag Week
Jun 13 – 16 US Open
Jun 13 – 20 National Hermit Week, National Nursing Assistants Week
Jun 16 – 22 National Craft Spirits Week
Jun 17 – 23 Meet a Mate Week, National Pollinator Week
Jun 18 – 22 England: Royal Ascot
Jun 21 – 27 Czech Days
Jun 22 – 23 ARRL Field Day
Jun 23 – 29 Lightning Safety Awareness Week (tentative)
Jun 24 – 30 Carpenter Ant Awareness Week
Jun 27 – Jul 4 Freedom Days
Jun 30 – Jul 4 National Tom Sawyer Days

DAILY HOLIDAYS

1. China: International Children's Day, GM Bankruptcy (10th Anniversary, 2009), *Heimlich Maneuver Day, Kenya: Madaraka Day, Malaysia: Head of State's Official Birthday, National

Trails Day, Samoa: Independence Day, Say Something Nice Day, Superman Day, United Nations: Global Day of Parents
2. Bhutan: Coronation Day, Israel: Jerusalem Day (Yom Yerushalayim), Italy: Republic Day, Italy: Wedding of the Sea, Marquis de Sade Birth (1740), National Cancer Survivors Day, National Gun Violence Awareness Day, Saint Erasmus Day, United Kingdom: Coronation Day, *Yell Fudge at the Cobras in North America Day (Don't laugh, I haven't seen any lately!)
3. *Chimborazo Day, Confederate Memorial Day, Ireland: June Bank Holiday, Japan: Day of the Rice God, *Mighty Casey Struck Out Day (1888), United Nations: World Bicycle Day, Zoot Suit Riots Anniversary (1943)
4. China: Tiananmen Square Massacre (1989), Finland: Flag Day, First Free Flight by a Woman (1784), Pulitzer Prize Day (1917), *United Nations: International Day of Innocent Children Victims of Aggression Day
5. *AIDS First Noted (1981), *Apple II (1977), Baby Boomers Recognition Day, Global Running Day, *United Nations: World Environment Day
6. *Bonza Bottler Day™, *D–Day (1944), *Drive in Movie Day (1933), Korea: Memorial Day, National Yo-yo Day, Prop 13 (40th Anniversary), *SEC Day (1934), Sweden: National Day, United Nations: Russian Language Day
7. Bahamas: Labor Day, *(Daniel) Boone Day, Korea: Tano Day, Mackintosh Day, Malta: National Day, National Donut Day, Supreme Court Strikes Down Connecticut Law Banning Contraception (1965)
8. American Heroine Woman Rewarded (1697), Belmont Stakes Day, National Caribbean-American HIV/AIDS Awareness Day, Shavout (begins at sundown), *United Nations: World Ocean Day, *Upsy Daisy Day, World Oceans Day
9. Children's Day in Massachusetts, Children's Sunday, *Donald Duck Day, International Archives Day, Pentecost, Whitsunday
10. *AA Day (1935), American Mint Day (1652), Congo: Brazzaville (Day of National Reconciliation), England: Dicing for Bibles, Portugal: Day of Portugal, Queen's Official Birthday (Selected Nations), Race Unity Day
11. Jacques Cousteau (1910), Germany: Waldchestag (Forest Day), *King Kamehameha Day (First Hawaiian King), Libya: Evacuation Day, National Call Your Doctor Day, National Cotton Candy Day
12. *Baseball's First Perfect Game (1880), First Man-Powered Flight Across English Channel (1979), Loving v Virginia Day (1967), National Jerky Day, Orlando Nightclub Massacre (2016), Paraguay: Peace with Bolivia Day, Philippines: Independence Day, Russia: Russia Day, *"Tear Down This Wall" Day, United Nations: World Day Against Child Labor
13. Roller Coaster Day (1884), United Nations: International Albinism Awareness Day
14. Alzheimer Day, *Family History Day, First Nonstop Transatlantic Flight (1919), First US Breach of Promise Day, *Flag Day, Japan: Rice Planting Festival, UNIVAC Computer Day, US Army Day, World Blood Donor Day
15. Longest Dam Race Day, *Magna Carta Day (1215), National Prune Day, Native American Citizenship Day, *Nature Photography Day, United Nations: World Elder Abuse Awareness Day, World Juggling Day
16. *Bloomsday, Father's Day, House Divided Speech (1858), Husband Caregiver Day, *Ladies' Day (Baseball), Orthodox Pentecost, South Africa: Youth Day, Trinity Sunday
17. *Apartheid Day, Bunker Hill Day, Quarterly Estimated Federal Income Tax Payers' Due Date (also Jan 15, Apr 15, and Sep 16, 2018), Iceland: Independence Day, *United Nations: World Day to Combat Desertification and Drought

18. Battle of Waterloo Day, Egypt: Evacuation Day, Seychelles: Constitution Day, United Nations: Sustainable Gastronomy Day
19. Belmont Stakes Day, *Garfield the Cat Day (1978), Lou Gehrig Day, *Juneteenth, Texas: Emancipation Day, United Nations: International Day for the Elimination of Sexual Violence in Conflict, Uruguay: Artigas Day, "War is Hell" Day (1879), *World Sauntering Day
20. Argentina: Flag Day, Corpus Christi *First Doctor of Science Earned by a Woman Day (1895), Recess at Work Day, *United Nations: World Refugee Day
21. Anne and Samantha Day (also Dec 21), Go Skateboarding Day, Greenland: National Holiday, Midsummer Day/Eve, Take Your Dog to Work Day®, United Nations: International Day of Yoga, World Music Day/Fête de la Musique
22. Great American Backyard Campout Day, Malta: Mnarja, Stupid Guy Thing Day, V-Mail Day (V-for Victory Day)
23. Corpus Christi (US Observance), Estonia: Victory Day, *Let It Go Day, Luxembourg: National Holiday, Orthodox Festival of All Saints, Runner's Selfie Day, Spain: Baby Jumping Festival Day, United Nations: International Widows Day, United Nations: Public Service Day
24. Canada: Discover Day (Newfoundland and Labrador), Canada: Saint John the Baptist Day, *Celebration of the Senses Day, China: Macau Day, "Flying Saucer" Day, Latvia: John's Day, Peru: Countryman's Day, Saint John the Baptist Day, Venezuela: Battle of Carabobo Day
25. Bhutan: National Day, Mozambique: Independence Day, National Columnists' Day, Slovenia: National Day, Supreme Court Ruling Day (Bans School Prayer, Upholds Rights to Die), Two Yugoslav Republics Declare Independence (1991), United Nations: Day of the Seafarer
26. *Barcode Day, CN Tower Day (1976), Federal Credit Union Act (1934), Human Genome Mapped (2000), Saint Lawrence Seaway Dedication (1959), Supreme Court Strikes Down Defense of Marriage Act (2013), United Nations Charter Signing (1945), *United Nations: International Day Against Drug Abuse and Illicit Trafficking, *United Nations: International Day in Support of Victims of Torture
27. *Decide to be Married Day, Djibouti: Independence Day, *Happy Birthday to "Happy Birthday to You" Day, Industrial Workers of the World Day, National Handshake Day, *National HIV Testing Day, PTSD Awareness Day, United Nations: Micro-, Small-, and Medium-Sized Enterprises Day
28. Monday Holiday Law (1968), National Eat at a Food Truck Day, Treaty of Versailles (100th Anniversary, 1919)
29. *Death Penalty Ban Day, Interstate Highway System Born (1956), Saint Peter and Paul Day, Saint Peter's Day, Seychelles: Independence Day, United Nations: International Day of the Tropics
30. Asteroid Day, Britain Cedes Claim to Hong Kong (1997), Charles Blondin's Conquest of Niagara Falls (1859), Congo: Independence Day, Gone with the Wind Published (1936), *Leap Second Adjustment Time Day, Log Cabin Day, *NOW (National Organization of Women) Founded (1966)

HOLIDAY MARKETING IDEAS FOR JUNE

International Men's Month — This has gone from a day to a week and is now a month-long celebration. There has to be a reason. and we, as people and business owners, need to make sure we are paying attention too. To celebrate this month why not create an event with the theme of "Giving Boys the Best Possible Start in Life", "Leading by Example", or any other number of other boy-to-men themes? I have found out in my research that there are themes assigned to this holiday every year since its inception in 1996.

Since you have a whole month to promote your business by helping to showcase the benefits that boys bring to life and the world there's no need to miss out on marketing by focusing on the males in our society.

Jun 11 National Call Your Doctor Day—Don't actually do this! That would drive the doctors to drink. LOL What you should do today is focus on helping others get their medical information together so that in case of emergency they are prepared. This is something we all need to do, make sure yours is up to date today and let someone know where they can find it or merely put it in your wallet. You can put together a card to give out to make it easy for folks to comply; and be sure to brand it so they know who to thank when the time comes. I have created one and placed it in the Samples appendix to help you get started sharing this all-important information.

Jun 17–23 National Pollinator Week—Have you ever thought about how important pollinators are to your very life? Insects of all sorts carry on the business of life mostly unobtrusively. So how do you have that same impact on your community? You might be surprised how significant an impact you are making. Nevertheless, teaching others how to affect their community in a positive way is a wonderful way to celebrate this week.

Whether you choose to support your community through training sessions or posting tips on your social media channels, every single act causes an effect. Wasn't that called the Butterfly Effect back a few years ago?

Jun28 National Eat at a Food Truck Day—Besides the obvious this weird and wacky holiday brings to mind the support of local businesses. I imagine a day spent with friends on a roaming food truck meal. What I envision is having the soup at one truck, going to another to crunch on a yummy salad, another to dine on the main course, and of course then there's dessert. How fun could that be? If you have kids, you might make it a day with them with you to make it a family fun day.

In previous years there were actually some food trucks that offer a 10% discount if you say the phrase, "Celebrate food trucks." when you step up to the window. For a list visit: https://itunes.apple.com/us/app/roaming-hunger-food-truck/id423850578?mt=8. If you used Uber, you could take advantage of the code "foodtruck16" to get a free ride (up to $20) to take you to each of the food trucks! Who knows, maybe they'll do it again this year? Visit www.neaftd.com to check it out.

There is a long list of big-boy networks and business that significantly impact our businesses and careers. So, today support the little guy or gal and shop locally or online with other small business owners.

While you are spending your day supporting other small- to mid-size or local businesses, a simple way to promote your own business is to share tweets or social media graphics. You'll find some tweets and graphics you can use in the Samples appendix. However, for a bit more fun, have your fans make a sign up and when they dine at the food truck(s) have them take a selfie to share on the net.

JULY

MONTH-LONG HOLIDAYS

Jul 3 – Aug 11 Dog Days
Jul 6 – Jul 28 Tour de France
Jul 26 – Aug 11 Pan American Games/Parapan AM Games 2019
Jul 3 – Aug 15 Air Conditioning Appreciation Days

Alopecia Month for Women, Bioterrorism/Disaster Education and Awareness Month, Cell Phone Courtesy Month, Herbal/Prescription Awareness Month, National Deli Salad Month, National "Doghouse Repairs" Month, National Grilling Month, National Horseradish Month, National Hot Dog Month, National Ice Cream Month, National Make a Difference to Children Month, National Minority Mental Health Awareness Month, National Recreation and Parks Month, National Vacation Rental Month, National Watermelon Month, Smart Irrigation Month, Women's Motorcycle Month, Worldwide Bereaved Parents Awareness Month

WEEK-LONG HOLIDAYS

Jul 4 – 10 Single Working Women's Week
Jul 7 – 13 Be Nice to Jersey Week
Jul 7 – 13 National Farrier's Week, Sports Cliché Week
Jul 7 – 14 Spain: Running of the Bulls
Jul 8 – 14 Nude Recreation Week
Jul 12 – 28 California State Fair (tentative)
Jul 18 – 21 Comic-Con International, Sloppy Joe's Hemingway® Look-alike Contest
Jul 18 – 25 Restless Leg Syndrome (RLS) Education and Awareness Week
Jul 19 – 27 North Dakota State Fair
Jul 20 – 28 National Moth Week
Jul 21 – 27 Captive Nations Week
Jul 24 – Aug 4 Ohio State Fair
Jul 26 – 28 Annie Oakley Days, Arcadia Daze
Jul 26 – Aug 4 Bangor State Fair
Jul 31 – Aug 1 Moby Dick Marathon

DAILY HOLIDAYS

1. Canada: Canada Day, Caribbean Day or Caricom Day, China: Half-year Day, *First Photographs Used in Newspaper Report (1848), *First Scheduled Television Broadcast (1941), Ghana: Republic Day, *IRS Day (1862), Medicare Day, Postage Stamp Day, Rwanda: Independence Day, Somalia Democratic Republic: National Day, Suriname: Liberation Day, Zamba: Heroes Day, *Zip Code Day, Zoo Day

2. Amelia Earhart Disappears (1937), *Civil Rights Day, *Constitution Day (USA), Declaration of Independence Resolution (1776), First Solo Round-the-World Balloon Flight (2002), Halfway Point of 2019, Zambia: Unity Day
3. Air-conditioning Appreciation Days, Belarus: Independence Day, *Canada: Quebec Founded (1608 *Compliment Your Mirror Day, *Stay Out of the Sun Day
4. *America the Beautiful Day, *Anne Landers (1918), Declaration of Independence Signing (1776), Earth at Aphelion Day, *Fourth of July or Independence Day, *Independence from Meat Day, India: Ratha Yatra, *Lou Gehrig Day (1939), Philippines: Fil-American Friendship Day
5. Algeria: Independence Day, *Bikini Day, Cape Verde: National Day, Isle of Man: Tynwald Day, *National Labor Relations Day, Slovakia: Saint Cyril and Methodius Day, Venezuela: Independence Day
6. Comoros: Independence Day, Czech Republic: Commemoration Day of Burning of John Hus, First Airship Crossing of the Atlantic (1919), Lithuania: Day of Statehood, Luxembourg: Ettelbruck Remembrance Day, Malawi: Republic Day, Name That Tune Day, Republican Party Day, *Take Your Webmaster to Lunch Day, United Nations: International Day of Cooperative
7. *Bonza Bottler Day™, Ducktona 500, *Father–Daughter Take a Walk Together Day, Japan: Tanabata (Star Festival), Solomon Islands: Independence Day, Spain: Running of the Bulls, Tanzania: Saba Saba Day, *Tell the Truth Day
8. Aspinwall Crosses US on Horseback (1911), International Town Criers Day, *SCUD Day (Savor the Comic, Unplug the Drama),
9. Argentina: Independence Day, First Open-Heart Surgery Day (1893), Morocco: Youth Day, South Sudan: Independence Day
10. Bahamas: Independence Day, *Clerihew Day, *Don't Step On a Bee Day, Martyrdom of the Bab
11. Bowdler's Day, *Day of the Five Billion, Make Your Own Sundae Day, Mongolia: Naadam National Holiday, Napalm Day, *United Nations: World Population Day
12. Bald is In Day, Family Feud Day (1976), Kiribati: Independence Day, National Motorcycle Day, Night of Nights, Northern Ireland: Orangemen's Day, São Tomé and Príncipe: Independence Day
13. Carver Day, *Embrace Your Geekness Day, France: Night Watch (La Retraite Aux Flambeaux, *Gruntled Workers Day, "Live Aid" Day, National Beef Tallow Day, National Nitrogen Ice Cream Day, Republic of Montenegro: National Day, Stone House Day, World Cup Day (1930)
14. Children's Party at Green Animals Day, England: Birmingham Riots Day (1791), France: Night Watch (Bastille Day)
15. Canada: *Saint Swithin's Day, Japan: Bon Odori (Feast of Lanterns) and Marine Day, Japan: Marine Day (Third Monday in July), National Get Out of the Doghouse Day, *Rembrandt Day, Saint Swithin's Day, United Nations: World Youth Skills Day
16. Atomic Bomb Test Day, Boliva: La Paz Day,
17. Astor Day, Disneyland Opened (1955), Korea: Constitution Day, Minimum Legal Drinking Age at 21 Day, Puerto Rico: Muñoz–Rivera Day, Take Your Poet to Work Day, World Emoji Day, "Wrong Way" Corrigan Day (1938)
18. Get to Know Your Customers Day (third Thursday of each quarter is set aside to get to know your customers even better), Mandela Day, Red Skelton Day (1913), United Nations: Nelson Mandela International Day

19. *Art Linkletter (1912), Elvis Presley First Single Day, Nicaragua: National Liberation Day, Saint Vincent de Paul Day
20. Columbia: Independence Day, Genva Accords (65th Anniversary, (1954), National Bridal Sale Day, National Woodie Wagon Day, Riot Act Day, *Special Olympics Day, Toss Away the "Could Haves" and "Should Haves" Day
21. Belgium: Independence Day, Fast of Tammuz, Guam: Liberation Day, *Hemingway Day (1899), Lowest Recorded Temperature Day (1983), National Ice Cream Day, No Pet Store Puppies Day
22. John Dillinger Day, *Pied Piper Day, *Rat–catchers Day, *Spooner's (Spoonerism) Day
23. Egypt: Revolution Day, *Hot Enough for Ya Day, Japan: Soma No Umaoi (Wild Horse Chasing)
24. Amelia Earhart Day, *Cousins Day, *National Drive-Thru Day, *National Tell an Old Joke Day, Pioneer Day
25. Costa Rica: Guanacast Day, First Airplane Crossing of English Channel (1909), Puerto Rico: Constitution Day, Spain: Saint James Day, Tunisia: Republic Day,
26. Americans with Disabilities Day, Armed Forces Unified (1947), Cuba: National Day (1953), Curaçao Day, *Esperanto Book Day, *George Bernard Shaw (1856), Liberia and Maldives: Independence Day, Potsdam Declaration (1945), *US Army Desegregation Day (1944)
27. *Atlantic Telegraph Day, *Insulin Isolated Day (1921), National Day of the Cowboy, *National Korean War Veterans Armistice Day, *Take Your Houseplant for a Walk Day, *Walk on Stilts Day
28. Auntie's Day, Beatrix Potter Day, Peru: Independence Day, Thailand: King's Birthday and National Day, World Hepatitis Day, World War I Begins (1914)
29. Global Tiger Day, Lord of the Rings Day, *NASA (1958), Rain Day,Spain: Festival of Near Death Experiences
30. Elvis Presley's First Concert (1954), *Emily Brontë (200th Anniversary), Henry Ford Day, National Chicken and Waffles Day, *Paperback Books (1935), United Nations: International Day of Friendship, United Nations: World Day Against Trafficking in Persons, Vanuatu: Independence Day
31. National Mutt Day, *US Patent Office Opened (1790)

HOLIDAY MARKETING IDEAS FOR JULY

Jul 7 Tell the Truth Day—Do we really need a day to remind us to tell the truth? It seems so. Therefore, today we celebrate everything honest and good. No white lies today, spend the whole day telling the truth, nothing but the truth, so help you God.

If you have little ones, teach them the importance of telling the truth. We are born knowing wrong. It's our job to teach them right and today is the perfect day to do just that.

There are some fun games you can play, one of which is to tell something about your life that others don't know and see if they can guess whether it is fact or fiction. That game and others like it could make for a fun event, if you are up to the challenge of hosting an honest bit of fun.

July 17 World Emoji Day—If you are up to the task today all your communications should be with emojis. I know that may be difficult, but it could be a belly of laughs too. If you can't get through the day and have to add text along with it, we'll all understand. But, be sure that you at least speak in hashtags on #worldemojiday to keep the laughter going. Why not create your own emoji and share it with the world? You never know, it might just become the next favorite emoji!

Jul 20 – 28 National Moth Week — Are you a Moth-er? Do you love everything about these fuzzy insects? This week might give you the heebee jeebies, or it may make you want to fly. No matter which side of the 'moth' you reside, today is a day to celebrate the diversity and beauty, yes beauty, of the moths all around us.

So, what can you do to celebrate National Moth week? Have a moth artwork contest and play some fun moth centered games. Or just get out there and help see if you just might find a brand-new species. There's always tweets and photos for sharing. Find your favorite moth and share the beauty by posting it on all your social media sites.

Jul 24 National Tell an Old Joke Day — I would bet you know at least one dumb old joke. Well, today is the day to share it and any others you have in your repertoire. Create a video or at least share your jokes on social media. If you have a particularly preposterous joke you might want to share it on a Facebook video. We'll all groan along with you.

You are always welcome to merely crate a graphic to share and you will find one in the Samples appendix to get your creative juices flowing. Be sure your joke graphic is specific to your business for extra impact. In my sample, since I am an author, I chose a genre specific joke and image for my graphic. You'll get the point when you see it. Oh, that was bad, but that's the theme of the day, eh?

AUGUST

MONTH-LONG HOLIDAYS

Aug 1 – 14 Dormition of Theotokos
Aug 2 – 10 Wales: National Eisteddfod of Wales
Aug 2 – 11 Strugis Rally
Aug 2 – 26 Scotland: Edinburgh International Festival
Aug 8 – 18 World Police and Fire Games: Chengdu 2019
Aug 24 – Oct 20 Maryland Renaissance Festival
Aug 26 – Sep 8 US Open Tennis Championship
American Adventures Month, Black Business Month, Boomers Making a Difference Month, Children's Eye Health and Safety Month, Children's Vision and Learning Month, International Pirate Month, National Immunization Awareness Month, National Spinal Muscular Atrophy Awareness Month, Read-A-Romance Month, Shop On-line for Groceries Month, What Will Be Your Legacy Month

WEEK-LONG HOLIDAYS

Aug 1 – 7 International Clown Week (First full week), National Minority Donor Awareness Week, World Breastfeeding Week
Aug 1 – 9 International Congress of Mathematicians 2018
Aug 1 – 11 Wisconsin State Fair (tentative)
Aug 2 – 4 Canada: Agrifair, National Czech Festival
Aug 2 – 10 Wales: National Eisteddfod of Wales
Aug 2 – 11 New Jersey State Fair/Sussex County Farm and Horse Show
Aug 2 – 18 Indiana State Fair
Aug 4 – 10 National Exercise with Your Child Week, Single Working Women's Week
Aug 5 – 9 Exhibitor Appreciation Week, Psychic Week
Aug 5 – 10 Old Fiddlers' Convention
Aug 8 – 11 National Hobo Days
Aug 8 – 17 Skowhegan State Fair
Aug 8 – 18 Illinois State Fair, Iowa State Fair, Missouri State Fair
Aug 9 – 11 Walt Whitman International Festival/Walt@200 Bicentennial Birthday Celebration
Aug 9 – 13 Perseid Meteor Showers
Aug 9 – 18 Elvis Week
Aug 10 – 17 England: Cowes Week
Aug 11 – 17 Assistance Dog Week
Aug 15 – 21 National Aviation Week
Aug 15 – 25 Kentucky State Fair (with World's Championship Horse Show), Little League Baseball® World Series
Aug 16 – 25 Western Idaho State Fair

Aug 16 – Sep 1 Finland: Helsinki Festival
Aug 17 – 22 Pittsburg Renaissance Fair
Aug 17 – 29 Minnesota Renaissance Festival
Aug 21 – Sep 32 New York State Fair
Aug 22 – Sep 2 Alaska State Fair, Maryland State Fair, Minnesota State Fair, Oregon State Fair
Aug 22 – 25 Hotter 'n Hell Hundred Bike Race
Aug 23 – Sep 2 Colorado State Fair, Nebraska State Fair
Aug 25 – 31 Be Kind to Humankind Week
Aug 29 – Sep 2 Blue Hill Fair, Louisiana Shrimp and Petroleum Festival and Fair, Payson Golden Onion Days, South Dakota State Fair
Aug 30 – Sep 2 Hog Capital of the World Festival, Odyssey — A Greek Festival, Washington State Fair, Woodstock Fair
Aug 30 – Sep 7 Eastern Idaho State Fair
Aug 31 – Sep 1 Totah Festival
Aug 31 – Sep 7 Cleveland National Air Show

DAILY HOLIDAYS

1. Benin: Independence Day, Emancipation of 500 Day, *Girlfriend's Day, *Lughnasadh, *Respect for Parents Day, Rounds Resounding Day, *Spiderman Day, Switzerland: Confederation Day, Trinidad and Tobago: Emancipation Day, United Kingdom: Minden Day, *US Census Day (1790), *US Customs Day, Word Lung Cancer Day, *World Wide Web or Internaut Day (1990)
2. Braham Pie Day, Costa Rica: Feast of Our Lady of Angels, *Declaration of Independence: Official Signing (1776), Macedonia: National Day
3. Amanday, Columbus Sails for the New World (1492), Equatorial Guinea: Armed Forces Day, Fancy Farm Picnic Day, Guinea-Bissau: Colonization Martyrs' Day, National Mustard Day, National Watermelon Day, Niger: Independence Day
4. American Family Day in Arizona, *Coast Guard Day, * Louis Armstrong Day, Queen Elizabeth Day, Single Working Woman's Day, Sister's Day®
5. Australia: Picnic Day, Bahamas: Emancipation Day, Burkina Faso: Republic Day, Canada: Civic Holiday, Colorado Day, Croatia: Homeland Thanksgiving Day, Grenada: Emancipatio Day, Iceland and Ireland: August Holiday, Jamaica: Independence Day, Scotland: Summer Bank Holiday
6. Bolivia: Independence Day, Death Penalty Day, *Hiroshima Day, Jamaica: Independence Day, National Night Out Day, Voting Rights Day (1965)
7. China: Double Seven Festival Day, Cote D'Ivoire: National Day, Hatfield-McCoy Feud Eruption Day, *Mata Hari Day (1876), National Lighthouse Day, *Particularly Preposterous Packaging Day, *Professional Speakers Day
8. *Bonza Bottler Day™, *Odie Day (1978), *Sneak Some Zucchini onto Your Neighbor's Porch Night, Tanzania: Farmers' Day, Wear Your Mother's Jewelry Day
9. Japan: Moment of Silence (Bombing of Nagasaki), *Moment of Silence Day, Singapore: National Day, South Africa: National Women's Day, *United Nations: International Day of The World's Indigenous People, *Veep Day
10. Candid Camera Day, Ecuador Independence Day, Middle Children's Day, National Garage Sale Day, National S'mores Day, Nestlé Day (1814), *Smithsonian Day, World Lion Day

11. *Alex Haley Day (1921), Chadd: Independence Day, Eid Al-Adha: Feast of Sacrifice, Herbert Hoover Day (Sunday nearest Aug 10th), Italy: Palio Del Golfo, Japan: Yama No Hi (Mountain Day), President's Joke Day, Saint Clare of Assisi: Feast Day, Tisha B'Av or Fast of Ab, Zimbabwe: Heroes Day
12. *Home Sewing Machine Day, *IBM PC Day, Night of the Murdered Poets, Thailand: Birthday of the Queen, *United Nations: International Youth Day, Victory Day, *Vinyl Record Day
13. *Alfred Hitchcock (1899), *Annie Oakley Day (1860), Bahamas: Fox Hill Day (second Tuesday in August), Berlin Wall Erected (1961), Central African Republic: Independence Day, *International Left Hander's Day, Lucy Stone Day (1818), Tunisia: Women's Day
14. *Navajo Nation: Code Talkers Day, Pakistan: Independence Day, *Social Security Day, V–J Day (1945)
15. *Assumption of the Virgin Mary, *Best Friends Day, *Chauvin Day, Check the Chip Day, China & Taiwan: Festival of the Hungry Ghosts, Congo (Brazzaville): National Day, Equatorial Guinea: Constitution Day, Hirohito's Radio Address (1945), India and Korea: Independence Day, Liechtenstein: National Day, *National Relaxation Day, *Panama Canal Day (1914), Transcontinental US Railway Completion (1870), *Woodstock (1969)
16. Dominican Republic: Restoration of the Republic, International Wave at Surveillance Day, Klondike Gold Discovery Day, National Roller Coaster Day
17. Balloon Crossing of Atlantic Ocean (1978), *Clinton's "Meaning of 'Is' Is" Day (1998), *Davy Crockett (1786), Gabon and Indonesia: Independence Day, International Geocaching Day, International Homeless Animals Day® and Candle-light Vigils, *Mae West Day (1893)
18. *Bad Poetry Day, *Birth Control Pills Day, *Mail–Order Catalog Day, National Badge Ribbon Day, Serendipity Day
19. Afghanistan: Independence Day (100th Anniversary), *Black Cow (Root Beer Float) Day, Canada: Yukon Discovery Day, Don Ho Day (1930), United Nations: World Humanitarian Day, World Photo Day
20. Hungary: Saint Stephen's Day, *Plutonium Day
21. Alexandria Library Sit-in Day, *American Bar Association Day, *Poet's Day, Seminole Tribe Day (1953), United Nations: International Day of Remembrance and Tribute to the Victims of Terrorism
22. *Be an Angel Day, *International Yacht Race Day, Vietnam Conflict Begins (1945)
23. First Man-Powered Flight (1977), Gene Kelly (1912), *Southern Hemisphere Hoodie-Hoo Day, *United Nations: Day for the Remembrance of the Slave Trade and Its Abolition, *Valentino Day
24. India: Krishna Janmashtami, International Bat Night, Liberia: Flag Day, *Pluto Demoted Day, Ukraine: Independence Day, *Vesuvius Day, William Wilberforce Day
25. Founders Day, *Kiss-and-Make-Up Day, *National Park Service Day, Uruguay: Independence Day, *Wizard of Oz Day (1939)
26. Baseball Day (First Televised, 1939), Hong Kong: Liberation Day, Nambia and Philippines: Heroes' Day, *National Dog Day, United Kingdom: Summer Bank Holiday, *Women's Equality Day
27. Moldova: Independence Day, *Mother Teresa Day, *"The Duchess" Who Wasn't Day
28. *March on Washington (1963), *Race Your Mouse Around the Icons Day, *Radio Commercials Day, Spain: La Tomatina (Tomato Food Fight Festival)
29. *According to Hoyle Day, Benton Neighbor Day, *More Herbs, Less Salt Day, Slovakia: National Uprising Day, United Nations: International Day Against Nuclear Tests

30. Huey P Long Day, Peru: Saint Rose of Lima Day, Turkey: Victory Day, United Nations: International Day of Victims of Enforced Disappearances
31. 2019 Burning Man Day, Islamic New Year, Kazakhstan and Kyrgyzstan: Constitution Day and Independence Day, *Love Litigating Lawyers Day, Malaysia: Freedom Day, Moldova: National Language Day, Trinidad and Tobago: Independence Day

HOLIDAY MARKETING IDEAS FOR AUGUST

International Pirate Month—Did you know it is International Pirate month? Arrrrr. Break out your best pirate language and have a bit of wholesome fun. This month, to showcase your business is as simple as sending out pirate cards and notes, both physical (these have a huge impact on the receiver since we don't get much but junk mail in the post) and digitally.

To add to the mix, you could host a pirate theme event. When you give your events a theme, it always draws (and quarters) more attention than a bland, join me for a seminar/webinar. Don't you agree?

Creating posters and table displays that are pirate oriented can add a bit of pizzazz to your room. If you can, you might even put footprints on the floor leading up to the event room and a big red X-marks the spot at the door when you have a live event.

I have placed a poster in the past in the Samples appendix that you are free to copy and use to market your event.

If you want to learn the truth about pirates, I highly recommend Robert Jacob's book, *A Pirate's Life in the Golden Age of Piracy*. In it he dispels the myths and reveals the truth about pirates and their lifestyles. Available at DocUmeantPublishing.com or at your local and online booksellers.

Aug 4 Single Working Woman's Day & Sister's Day®—Interestingly enough this one covers just about every female alive, as we are either working or a sister or maybe both. So, as you think about how to market your business on a day that's geared specifically in celebration of women consider their needs. How can you help them succeed and know they are appreciated and loved?

Let's think about the small things we can do, since it is said that it's the small gifts that matter the most. Sending notes in the mail can be done a head of the day and then today you might consider hosting a party or even teaching event. When you share information that others want and need, they appreciate and notice you—today is your chance to share.

Cards and social media always work, but live events are where you make the most headway in business marketing. Your events don't always have to be informational, they can just be a gathering of friends. However, rubbing elbows and showing you care will make all the difference when it comes time to hire someone that does or has something another person needs. So, get out there and share with your sisters, rub elbows, and share the love!

Aug 16 International Wave at Surveillance Day — The man is watching! I don't know about your town, but in mine we have surveillance cameras almost on every corner. How do I know? I recently got a ticket in the mail when there was nobody on the street but me! Agh! So, when I noticed we have a weird and wacky holiday that features our nosy government I just had to focus on it.

Wave at every camera as you go through the intersections of life. Whether that juncture in the road is filled with roadblocks or provides clear sailing, be thankful for the opportunity to challenge yourself as you move forward on the road to success.

Gather a group of likeminded friends and create a mastermind group to help you bounce ideas around and get inspiration to keep you moving in the right direction. Or, just focus on social media sharing your wave to the future. You'll find a graphic that you can use to pave the way to a fun and rewarding 'Wave at Surveillance Day'.

Aug 28 Spain: La Tomatina — The world's biggest food fight, now that looks like good 'ol fun! Well, maybe not. At any rate, it is a fairly new weird and wacky holiday.

Figure 1 By flydime - La Tomatina (25.08.2010) / Spain, Buñol, CC BY-SA 2.0, https://commons.wikimedia.org/w/index.php?curid=11911123 It's a reason to have some good ol' fun!

How to use it to market your business is a very good question indeed. I'm not suggesting you have a food fight however tempted you are. Perhaps you might consider cooking classes, or tomato recipe swaps, or maybe even sharing a video on cooking a tomato dish. All of these are fine ideas, just be sure not to forget to add your brand to anything you prepare.

SEPTEMBER

MONTH-LONG HOLIDAYS

Sep 5 – 15 Canada: Toronto International Film Festival
Sep 15 – Oct 15 National Hispanic Heritage Month
Sep 12 – 29 England: The Big E
Sep 20 – Nov 2 Danger Run
Sep 21 – Oct 6 Oktoberfest
Sep 22 – 28 Banned Books Week — Celebrating the Freedom to Read

Atrial Fibrillation Month, Attention Deficit Disorder Month, Be Kind To Editors and Writers Month, Childhood Cancer Awareness Month, Chili: National Month, Fall Hat Month, Great American Low–Cholesterol, Low-fat Pizza Bake Month, Gynecology Cancer Awareness Month, Happy Cat Month, Hunger Action Month, Library Card Sign-up Month, National DNA, Genomics and Stem Cell Education Month, National Head Lice Prevention Month, National Honey Month, National Mushroom Month, National Preparedness Month, National Recovery Month, National Rice Month, National Service Dog Month, National Skin Care Awareness Month, One-on-One Month, Ovarian Cancer Awareness Month, Pleasure Your Mate Month, Scandinavian Fest Day, September is Healthy Aging® Month, Shameless Promotion Month, Sports Eye Health and Safety Month, Subliminal Communications Month, Update Your Resume Month, Whole Grains Month, Worldwide Speak Out Month

WEEK-LONG HOLIDAYS

Sep 1 – 7 Brazil: Independence Week, National Waffle Week
Sep 2 – 5 Great Fire of London (1666)
Sep 2 – 6 National Payroll Week
Sep 5 – 8 Longs Peak Scottish/Irish Highland Festival
Sep 3 – 7 Play Days
Sep 5 – 15 New Mexico State Fair (tentative), Utah State Fair
Sep 6 – 15 Kansas State Fair, Tennessee State Fair
Sep 7 – 8 Sodbuster Days
Sep 7 – 14 Southeastern Missouri District Fair
Sep 9 – 13 Substitute Teacher Appreciation Week
Sep 9 – 14 National Line Dance Week
Sep 12 – 15 Hummingbird Celebration, Newport International Boat Show
Sep 12 – 22 Oklahoma State Fair
Sep 15 – 21 Build a Better Image Week, National Farm Safety and Health Week, National Historically Black Colleges and Universities Week (tentative), National Rehabilitation Awareness Celebration Week, National Singles Week, Prostate Cancer Awareness Week, United Kingdom: Battle of Britain Week

Sep 17 – 23 Constitution Week
Sep 18 – 22 National Guitar Flat-picking Championships and Valley Festival
Sep 20 – Nov 2 Rugby World Cup
Sep 22 – 28 Banned Books Week — Celebrating the Freedom to Read, Tolkien Week, World Rabies Day, World Reflexology Week
Sep 23 – 28 International Week of the Deaf
Sep 23 – 29 International Women's Ecommerce Days
Sep 27 – 29 Baltimore Book Festival
Sep 27 – Oct 6 Virginia State Fair
Sep 27 – Oct 20 Texas State Fair

DAILY HOLIDAYS

1. Chicken Boy's Birthday, *Edgar Rice Burroughs (1875) *Emma M. Nutt Day, International Toy Tips Executive Toy Test Day, Italy: Historical Regatta and Joust of the Saracen, Japan: Kanto Earthquake Memorial Day, Orthodox Ecclesiastical New Year, Slovakia: Constitution Day, Titanic Discovery Day, Uzbekistan: Independence Day, WWII Begins (1939)
2. Calendar Adjustment Day, Canada and US: Labor Day (first Monday in September), Mouthguard Day, US Treasury Department Founded Day, Vietnam: Independence Day, *V–J Day
3. Penny Press Day (1833), Qatar: Independence Day, San Marino: National Day
4. Curaçao: Animal's Day, Electric Lights Day, Earth Hour, *Newspaper Carrier Day, *Paul Harvey Day
5. Jesse James Day (1847), Michigan's Great Fire of 1881, United Nations: International Day of Charity
6. Baltic States: Independence Day, Bring Your Manners to Work Day, Bulgaria: Unification Day, Jane Addams Day, National Day of Prayer and Remembrance, National Dog Walker Appreciation Day, Pakistan: Defense of Pakistan Day, Swaziland: Independence Day, United Nations: Millennium Summit (1955)
7. Brazil: Independence Day, *Google Commemoration Day (1998), *Grandma Moses Day, *Neither Snow nor Rain Day–Day, Queen Elizabeth I Birthday (1533)
8. Andorra: National Holiday, Huey P. Long Shot Day, Macedonia: Independence Day, Malta: Victory Day, National Grandparents' Day, Pediatric Hematology/Oncology Nurses Day, Star Trek Day, Tarzan Day, *United Nations: International Literacy Day
9. Ashura: Tenth Day, *Bonza Bottler Day™, Japan: Chrysanthemum Day, Korea, Democratic People's Republic of: National Day, Luxembourgh: Liberation Ceremony, National Boss/Employee Exchange Day, Tajikistan: Independence Day, *Wonderful Weirdos Day
10. Belize: Saint George's Caye Day, China: Teacher's Day, Swap Ideas Day, World Suicide Prevention Day
11. *Attack on America Day, Catalonia: National Day of Catalonia, Ethiopia: New Year's Day, *Food Stamps Day, *Patriot Day and National Day of Service and Remembrance
12. Defenders Day, Guinea-Bissau: National Holiday, United Nations: Day for South-South Cooperation, Video Games Day
13. Blame Someone Else Day, Friday the 13th, Kids Take Over the Kitchen Day, Korean: Chusok, *National Celiac Awareness Day, Roald Dahl Day, Scooby Doo Day
14. Gravitational Waves First Detected (2015), Prairie Day, *Solo Transatlantic Balloon Crossing (1984)

15. *Agatha Christie Day, Costa Rica and El Salvador: Independence Day, *First National Convention for Blacks (1830), *Greenpeace Day (1971), Guatemala and Honduras: Independence Day, International Red Panda Day, Nicaragua: Independence Day, *United Nations: International Day of Democracy
16. *Anne Bradstreet Day, Cherokee Strip Day, General Motors Day, *Great Seal of the US (1782), Japan: Respect for the Aged Day, Mayflower Day, Mexico: Independence Day, Papua New Guinea: Independence Day, Quarterly Estimated Federal Income Tax Payers' Due Date (also Jan 15, Apr 15, and June 17, 2018), *United Nations: International Day for the Preservation of the Ozone Layer, World Play-Doh Day
17. Angola: Day of the National Hero,*Citizenship Day, *Constitution Day (1787), IT Professionals Day, National Constitution Center Constitution Day, National Football League Formed Day (1920), Netherlands: Prinsjesdag, United Nations: Opening Day of General Assembly, VFW Ladies Auxiliary Day
18. Chili: Independence Day, National Cheeseburger Day, National HIV/AIDS and Aging Awareness Day, National School Backpack Awareness Day, *US Air Force Birthday, *US Capitol Cornerstone Laid, US Takes Out its First Loan (1789), White Woman Made American Indian Chief Day
19. *"Iceman" Mummy Discovered (1991), *International Talk Like a Pirate Day, Saint Christopher (Saint Kitts) and Nevis: Independence Day
20. *Billie Jean King Wins Battle of the Sexes (1973), Financial Panic Day, Fonzie Jumps the Shark Day, *National Equal Rights Founded (1884), National POW/MIA Recognition (the third Friday in September), National Tradesmen Day
21. Armenia, Belize and Malta: Independence Day, International Coastal Cleanup, International Red Panda Day, Locate and Old Friend Day, Malta: Independence Day, National Surgical Technologists Day, *United Nations: International Day of Peace
22. American Business Woman's Day, Dear Diary Day, *Emancipation Proclamation (1862), Hobbit Day, Ice Cream Cone Day, International Day of Radiant Peace, Long Count Day (1927), Mali: Independence Day, National Centenarian's Day, National Walk 'n' Roll Dog Day, Remote Employee Appreciation Day, US Postmaster General's Day (1789)
23. Baseball's Greatest Dispute Day, *Celebrate Bisexuality Day, Checkers Day, Family Day—Making Everyday Special Day, Japan: Autumnal Equinox Day, *Lewis and Clark Expedition Returns (1806), Mabon (Alban Elfed), Planet Neptune Discovery (1846), Saudi Arabia: Kingdom Unification, United Nations: International Day of Sign
24. Cambodia: Constitutional Declaration Day, Daniel Boone Day, Guinea-Bissau: Independence Day, Innergize Day, Mozambique: Armed Forces Day, *National Punctuation Day, Schwenkfelder Thanksgiving, South Africa: Heritage Day
25. *First American Newspaper Published (1690), *Greenwich Mean Time Begins (1676), National Psychotherapy Day, National Women's Health and Fitness Day, Pacific Ocean Discovered (1513) Rwanda: Republic Day
26. *Johnny Appleseed Day, First Televised Presidential Debate (1960), Remember Me Thursday, United Nations: World Maritime Day
27. *Samuel Adams (1722), *Ancestor Appreciation Day, Buffalo Roundup, Ethiopia: True Cross Day, Hug a Vegan Day, Saint Vincent DePaul Feast Day, *World Tourism Day
28. *Cabrillo Day, Fish Amnesty Day, National Public Lands Day, R.E.A.D. in America Day, Taiwan: Confucius and Teachers' Day, United Nations/UNESCO: International Day for Universal Access to Information, World Rabies Day

29. Michelangelo Antonio (1912), Gold Star Mother's and Family Day (always the last Sunday in September), International Day of the Deaf, Michaelmas, *National Attend Your Grandchild's Birth Day, National Biscotti Day, National Coffee Day, Paragiau" Boquerón day, Rosh Hashanah (begins at sundown), Scotland Yard Day (1829), Veterans of Foreign Wars Day
30. Botswana: Independence Day, First Criminal Execution in America Day (1630), Gutenberg Bible Published (1452), International Translation Day, Saint Jerome: Feast Day

HOLIDAY MARKETING IDEAS FOR SEPTEMBER

Attention Deficit Disorder Month—Do you have trouble focusing to the end of a project? I think we all must to some degree. How can we keep our focus and stay on task? Perhaps there are business owners out there who could share some insights with the rest of us.

Besides the tried and true social media, there's a good chance you would have a great turnout if you either hosted or sponsored a once weekly event. Since this weird and wacky holiday is a month-long adventure so too should your event. While I'm not suggesting you attempt a daily event for a whole month, once a week for an hour or so might be the perfect solution to keep the audience's from losing focus along the way.

Gather speakers who can share some solutions to this issue and play some games that will train the brain while you are at it. Don't go all technical on them, unless your group is made up of doctors, focus on solutions and the positive aspects. Goal setting might be another aspect as well as time management. There are a few ideas to get you started. It's up to you to take it from here.

Sep 4 Earth Hour—This idea behind Earth Hour is that between 8:30 and 9:30 p.m. we are to turn off all non-essential lights. A lightbulb of an idea to promote your business is to spend the day speaking about what it would be like to have to go without electricity for a day. How would it impact your business and your life? Would your business die a sudden death or are you prepared for that catastrophic disaster should it occur?

It's time to re-evaluate your business and create your preparedness plan. Not only if the lights went out, but if something should happen to you that you couldn't sustain your business. Open up this all-important conversation with your staff or team and map out a plan for 'just in case'.

Talk to other business owners and work together to brainstorm ideas. Have a seminar or webinar and bring in someone savvy in this area of expertise, a lawyer is a good place to start searching for a speaker, then look to technical savvy personnel who might give you an insight on how to prepare for and work around this issue. In the Samples appendix is a flyer you can customize and use to promote your event.

Social media tips and tweets are simple ideas you can do if you aren't able to host or run a seminar/webinar. At the very least share a note or card to your very best customers and clients, wishing them a Happy Earth Hour Day with a reminder to turn off those lights for an hour at 8:30 p.m.

Lights out!

Sep 15–21 Build a Better Image Week—Coming up with ideas on how to market your business this week should be a simple task. We all need to feel better to look better. That opens the businesses that could benefit from marketing their wares this week to not only physical aspects of a better image but also to mental ones as well. Start by sharing tips in tweets and social media and offer up a handout that can be downloaded from your website with just a bit more information.

Your tips and tweets should end with a CTA (call to action) to download your freebee. When they get to your website be sure to capture their email address and name to help build your contact list.

Even designers and graphic artists can share on design. While an interior designer might share before and after of their work, a graphic artist, book designer or other artistically enabled artists might share techniques to take your work from okay to wow!

As you can see, there is much room for exploration and ideas for us all to sit up and take notice. Sure, you can always fall back on social media, but why not take it just a little step further. You have a whole week to get it done. Don't let it pass you by.

Sep 20 Fonzie Jumps the Shark Day—The idiom "jumping the shark" is pejorative, most commonly used in reference to unsuccessful gimmicks for promoting something. So, to me that means that there are times in our businesses that we need to let go and move on. Are you still holding on to ideas and plans that have long since stopped being effective? Does the term doing things the same way and getting the same results feel relative? Is this not just another way of saying 'running around in circles'?

This weird and wacky holiday consider expanding your horizons. Look for new products or services you can provide. When you take the time to send out customer surveys, they will tell you want they want and need, then you merely need to answer that need. Growing your business and help others at the same time is always a win-win.

OCTOBER

MONTH-LONG HOLIDAYS

Oct 10 – 20 Arkansas State Fair and Livestock Show
Oct 24 – Nov 11 World Origami Days
Oct 29 Rabi'i: The Month of Migration (begins)

Adopt A Shelter Dog Month, American Cheese Month, Antidepressant Death Awareness Month, Breast Cancer Awareness Month, Celebrating the Bi-lingual Child Month, Celiac Disease Awareness Month, Contact Lens Safety Month, Co-op Awareness Month, Domestic Violence Awareness Month, Dyslexia Awareness Month, Emotional Intelligence Month, Gay and Lesbian History Month, German-American Heritage Month, Global Diversity Awareness Month, Go Hog Wild — Eat Country Ham Month, Health Literacy Month, National Audiology Awareness Month, National Breast Cancer Awareness Month, National Bullying Prevention Awareness Month, National Chiropractic Month, National Crime Prevention Month, National Cyber Security Awareness Month, National Dental Hygiene Month, National Depression Education and Awareness Month, National Disability Employment Awareness Month, National Domestic Violence Awareness Month, National Down Syndrome Awareness Month, National Kitchen and Bath Month, National Liver Awareness Month, National Medical Librarian Month, National Orthodontic Health Month, National Physical Therapy Month, National Popcorn Poppin' Month, National Reading Group Month, National Roller Skating Month, National Seafood Month, National Spina Bifida Awareness Month, National Stamp Collecting Month, National Stop Bullying Month, National Work and Family Month, Organize Your Medical Information Month, Polish American Heritage Month, Positive Attitude Month, Rett Syndrome Awareness Month, Squirrel Awareness and Appreciation Month, Talk About Prescriptions Month, Vegetarian Awareness Month, World Menopause Month

WEEK-LONG HOLIDAYS

Oct 2 – 6 England: Nottingham Goose Fair
Oct 2 – 13 Mississippi State Fair
Oct 3 – 13 Georgia National Fair
Oct 4 – 10 United Nations: World Space Week
Oct 4 – 27 Arizona State Fair
Oct 5 – 13 Albuquerque International Balloon Fiesta,
Oct 5 – 13 Albuquerque International Balloon Fiesta
Oct 5 – 26 Spain: Semana Cervantina (Cervantes Week)
Oct 6 – 12 Emergency Nurses Week, Fire Prevention Week, Getting the World to Beat a Path to Your Door Week, Mental Illness Awareness Week, National Carry a Tune Week, National Metric Week
Oct 7 – 11 National Heimlich Heroes Week

Oct 9–20 South Carolina State Fair
Oct 10–17 Take Your Medicine Americans Week
Oct 10–20 Arkansas State Fair and Livestock Show
Oct 11–19 Canada: Kitchener-Waterloo Oktoberfest
Oct 11–13 Apple Butter Makin' Days, Southern Festival of Books: A Celebration of the Written Word
Oct 12–14 Chowder Days
Oct 13–19 Bullying Bystanders Unite Week, Earth Science Week, National Food Bank Week, Teen Read Week™
Oct 13–26 Brazil: Cirio De Nazare
Oct 14–15 National School Lunch Week, Nuclear Science Week
Oct 15–20 Japan: Newspaper Week
Oct 16–20 Germany: Frankfurt Book Fair
Oct 17–24 Food and Drug Interaction Education and Awareness Week
Oct 17–27 North Carolina State Fair
Oct 18–20 Missouri Day Festival, Philippines: Masskara Festival
Oct 20–26 National Character Counts Week, National Chemistry Week, National Forest Products Week, Rodent Awareness Week, Spiritual Care Week
Oct 24–30 United Nations: Disarmament Week
Oct 24–31 Prescription Errors Education and Awareness Week
Oct 24–Nov 10 Louisiana State Fair
Oct 25–31 International Magic Week

DAILY HOLIDAYS

1. China, People's Republic of: National Day: 70th Founding, Cyberspace Day, Cyprus: Independence Day, *Fire Pup Day, Living Dead Day, Model-T Day, Nigeria: Independence Day, South Korea: Armed Forces Day, This is Your Life Day, Tuvalu: Independence Day, US 2020 Federal Fiscal Year Begins, World Vegetarian Day
2. Gandhi (150th Birthday), *Guardian Angels Day, *Groucho Marx (1890), Guinea: Independence Day, *National Custodial Workers Day, *"Peanuts" Debut Day (1950), United Nations: International Day of Nonviolence, World Day for Farmed Animals
3. Captain Kangaroo Day, Germany: Day of German Unity, Honduras: Francisco Morazán Holiday, Korea: Tangun Day (National Foundation Day), *Mickey Mouse Club Day (1955), Netherlands: Relief of Leiden Day, United Kingdom: National Poetry Day
4. *Dick Tracy Day (1931), *Georgian Calendar Adjustment Day, International Ships-In-Bottles Day, Kids Music Day, Lesotho: Independence Day, National Diversity Day, National Taco Day, Saint Francis of Assisi: Feast Day, *Ten-Four Day, World Smile Day
5. Chic Spy Day™, Fall Astronomy Day, James Bond Day, Portugal: Republic Day, *United Nations: World Teachers Day, Woofstock
6. *American Library Association Founding Day (1876), Blessing of the Fishing Fleet, Country Inn, Bed-and-Breakfast Day Egypt: Armed Forces Day, Ireland: Ivy Day, *Jackie Mayer Rehab Day, *National German-American Day, National G.O.E. (Growth.Overcome.Empower.) Day, National Noodle Day, World Communion Sunday, Yom Kippur War
7. Blue Shirt Day™/World Day of Bullying Prevention™, China: Chung Yeung Festival (Double Nine Day), Child Health Day (always issued for the first Monday in October), National Forgiveness and Happiness Day, United Nations: World Habitat Day

8. Ada Lovelace Day, *Alvin C. York Day, Croatia: Statehood Day, *Great Chicago Fire (1871), India: Dasara (Dussehra), International Face Your Fears Day, National Hydrogen and Fuel Cell Day, National Pierogy Day, National Salmon Day, Peshtigo Forest Fire (1871), World Child Development Day, Yom Kippur (begins at sundown)
9. Emergency Nurses Day, *Leif Erickson Day, International Top Spinning Day, Korea: Hangul (Alphabet Day), National Bring Your Teddy Bear to Work Day, National Bullying Prevention Day, National Nanotechnology day, Peru: Day of National Honor, Uganda: Independence Day, *United Nations: World Post Day
10. *Bonza Bottler Day™, *Double 10 Day, Motorsport Memorial Day, National Handbag Day, *Tuxedo Day, *US Naval Academy Day, World Day Against the Death Penalty, *World Mental Health Day
11. *Adding Machine Day, *General Pulaski Memorial Day, *National Coming Out Day, Southern Food Heritage Day, United Nations: International Day of the Girl Child
12. Bahamas Discovery Day, Columbus Day (Traditional), *Day of the Six-Billion, Equatorial Guinea: Independence Day, *International Moment of Frustration Scream Day, Mexico: Dia de la Raza, Monster Myths by Moonlight, Spain: National Holiday, Universal Music Day
13. *Jesse Leroy Brown Day, Grandmother's Day in Florida, *Navy Birthday, Samoa and American Samoa: White Sunday, Sukkot (begins at sundown), United Nations: International Day for Natural Disaster Reduction. Whitehouse Cornerstone Laid (1792)
14. *Be Bald and Be Free Day, American Indian Heritage Day (Alabama), Canada: Thanksgiving Day, Columbus Day (Observed and Traditional), Discovery Day in Hawaii, Fiji: Independence Day, Japan: Health-Sports Day, National Kick Butt Day, Native Americans' Day (South Dakota), Sound Barrier Broken (1947), Supersonic Skydive Day, (2012), Virgin Islands-Puerto Rico Friendship Day, Yorktown Victory Day
15. *Blind Americans Equality Day (formerly White Cane Safety Day), First Manned Flight (1783), National Cake Decorating Day, National Grouch Day, National Latino AIDS Awareness Day, United Nations: International Day of Rural Women
16. Birth Control Day (1916), Dictionary Day, Global Cat Day, Hagfish Day, Million Man March (1995), Missouri Day, *National Boss' Day, National Fossil Day, United Nations: World Food Day
17. 300 Millionth American Born (2006), Black Poetry Day, Get Smart About Credit Day, Evel Knievel Day, Get to Know Your Customers Day (third Thursday of each quarter is set aside to get to know your customers even better),*Mulligan Day, National Depression Screening Day, National Playing Card Collection Day, San Francisco 1989 Earthquake (1989), *United Nations: International Day for the Eradication of Poverty
18. Alaska Day, Azerbaijan: Independence Day, Canada: Persons Day (90th Anniversary, 1929), Comic Strip Day, National Mammography Day, Saint Luke Feast Day, Water Pollution Control Day, *World Menopause Day
19. Bridge Day, Evaluate Your Life Day, LGBT Center Awareness Day, Sweetest Day, Yorktown Day
20. AIDS Walk Atlanta and 5K Run, John Dewey Day, Guatemala: Revolution Day, Kenya: Mashujaa Day, Miss America Rose Day
21. *Incandescent Lamp Day, Jamaica: National Heroes Day, Shemini Atzeret, Taiwan: Overseas Chinese day, Virgin Islands: Hurricane Thanksgiving Day
22. *International Stuttering Awareness Day, Simchat Torah, Smart is Cool Day, World's End Day

23. Hungary: Republic Day (Declares Independence), *IPod Day, National Mole Day, Swallows Depart from San Juan Capistrano, Thailand: Chulalongkorn Day
24. First Barrel Jump over Niagara Falls (1901), Recycle Your Mercury Thermostat Day, United Nations Day, *United Nations: World Development Information Day
25. First Female FBI Agents (1972), Frankenstein Friday, Picasso Day, Saint Crispin's Day, Sourest Day, Taiwan: Retrocession Day
26. Austria: National Day, Erie Canal Day, Gunfight at the O.K. Corral (1881), Mule Day
27. *Cranky Coworkers Day, European Union: Daylight Savings Time Ends, India: Diwali (Deepavali), Mother-in-Law Day, *Navy Day, Reformation Sunday Saint Vincent and the Grenadines: Independence Day, Turkmenistan: Independence Day, United Nations: World Day for Audiovisual Heritage, *Walt Disney Day
28. Czech Republic: Independence Day, Greece: Ochi Day, Ireland: October Bank Holiday, New Zealand: Labor Day, *Saint Jude's Day, Statue of Liberty Dedication (1886), Zambia: Independence Day
29. Birth of Bab, *Internet Created (50th Anniversary, 1969), National Cat Day, Turkey: Republic Day
30. Birth of Baha'u'llah (1817), Checklists Day, *Create A Great Funeral Day, Devil's Night, *Emily Post Day, *Haunted Refrigerator Night, National Candy Corn Day, "War of the Worlds" (1938) World Audio Drama Day
31. *Books for Treats Day, *Halloween, *Magic Day, Mount Rushmore Day, *National Knock–Knock Day, *Reformation Day, Samhain, Taiwan: Chiang Kai-Shek Day, Trick or Treat or Beggar's Night, United Nations: World Cities Day

HOLIDAY MARKETING IDEAS FOR OCTOBER

Positive Attitude Month — Now there's a month to celebrate! Since you have a whole month to appreciate the good things in life and business you have plenty of time to focus your events and other offerings. Start off with the simple and, if you are up to the task, add in additional more complex events.

Posting positive tweets and other social media posts can be done as often as you can schedule them. At least once a day for quotes would be good. If you want to take it up a notch you could also turn them into graphics to share. You'll find a list of positive quotes in the Samples appendix that you can use for this task or you can find some of your favorites with a quick search of any quote index.

Then, cards and email would come next. Remember, that snail mail cards have much more impact than emails. Adjust your marketing accordingly.

Finally, are events. A good ol' webinar, seminar, Facebook Live, Google Hangout can be scheduled with one topic for an hour each week throughout the month. Ideas on topic matter could vary from overcoming challenges to dress for success principles. Public speaking training is another fine option. Then there is body language and the lessons to learn that would make a positive impact even in one-on-one meetings. These are just a few to get your creative juices flowing.

Oct 1 This is Your Life Day — I'm thinking that a terrific way to celebrate this weird and wacky holiday would be to gather a group of your clients and customers together and get to know each other better. Another idea is to run an essay contest and the winner could get some valuable prizes as you celebrate their life and accomplishments. If you choose to do this, you may want to seek out sponsors and sponsor gifts to make the day extra special. Then be sure to let the media know, they love this sort of 'feel good' story.

Oct 4 National Taco Day — Today, as a nation we celebrate everything Mexican, especially the national food, the taco. Whether you prefer the crunchy American taco or the authentic Mexican soft taco, this is a source of all the main food list items in one neat package. You can get them mild or spicy, or even extra hot! The variety is nearly endless.

In observance of National Taco Day, start with recipe swaps and consider ether making coloring pages available (branded of course) or holding a coloring contest. Share pictures and tell the stories behind them of events where tacos were or are the main dish being served. You'll find a coloring page in the Samples appendix if you need one.

Oct 13 Jesse Leroy Brown Day — Today commemorates the first black American naval aviator who just happens to be the first black naval officer to lose his life in combat. He was shot down over Korea on Dec 4, 1950. He even had a naval ship named in his honor; the USS Jesse L Brown. I would say a man who made his mark so deeply in society deserves recognition. He broke not only one barrier for African-Americans but three, as he was the first black naval officer ever to be honored by having a commissioned ship with his name on it. That ship was later decommissioned in 1994. But, what an accomplishment in one lifetime.

So, to honor Jesse Leroy Brown send out cards and social media posts that you, of course, have branded to your business. If you enjoy hosting events yours could focus on helping others up the ladder to success. Find out ahead of time what their needs are with a simple survey and then plan your event around the answers.

If you decide to host a live event, may I suggest you offer your classes or seminar to those in your community who need the information. Things like how to dress for an interview, how to fill out a resume, how to prepare for the job market, etc., might be a very good start. Then let the media know and you are sure to get their attention.

Oct 25 Picasso Day — Do I see a budding artist in the room? How fun this day could be when celebrating the arts? Consider taking a group of seniors to the art gallery, or if you are up to it, young budding artists. If you get a group of business owners to do the same and let the media know they will paint a pretty picture of your businesses and efforts. Imagine each business represented being interviewed? Would that not do good things for your businesses?

Again, coloring pages would be sufficient, branded of course, or perhaps a contest might be in order. An art walk featuring local artists might be a good idea.

At the very least, post some of your own art on your social media while mentioning that they are in honor of Picasso Day. With all the adult coloring books coming out now, you're sure to find your own artistic style. You don't have any? I'd say it's about time for you to start.

NOVEMBER

MONTH-LONG HOLIDAYS

Nov 21 – Dec 30 Germany: Duisburg Christmas Market
Nov 23 – Dec 1 Mexico: Guadalajara International Book Fair
Nov 25 – Dec 23 Germany: Frankfurt Christmas Market

American Diabetes Month, Aviation History Month, Banana Pudding Lovers Month, Diabetic Eye Disease Month, Eye Donation Month, Lung Cancer Awareness Month, Movember, National Adoption Month, National Alzheimer's Disease Awareness Month, National Diabetes Month, National Epilepsy Awareness Month, National Family Caregivers Month, National Georgia Pecan Month, National Inspirational Role Models Month, National Long-Term Care Awareness Month, National Marrow Awareness Month, National Medical Science Liaison Awareness and Appreciation Month, National Native American Heritage Month, National Novel Writing Month, National Runaway Prevention Month, Peanut Butter Lovers Month, Picture Book Month, PPSI AIDS Awareness Month, Prematurity Awareness Month, Vegan Month, Worldwide Bereaved Siblings Month

WEEK-LONG HOLIDAYS

Nov 4 – 8 National Patient Accessibility Week, National Young Reader's Week
Nov 10 – 16 Snowcare for Troops Awareness Week
Nov 11 – 23 International Games Week™
Nov 15 – 17 National Donor Sabbath
Nov 18 – 22 American Education Week
Nov 24 – 30 National Family Week, National Game & Puzzle Week
Nov 25 – 30 Better Conversation Week

DAILY HOLIDAYS

1. Algeria: Revolution Day, *All Hallows or All Saints Day, Antigua and Barbuda: Independence Day, European Union (1993), Extra Mile Day, Hockey Mask Day, Lisbon Earthquake (1755), Mexico: Day of the Dead, *National Authors' Day, National Medical Science Liaison (MSL) Awareness and Appreciation Day, National Sports Fan Day, Samoa: Arbor Day
2. *All Souls Day, Daniel Boone Day, *First Scheduled Radio Broadcast (1920), National Bison Day, Pumpkin Destruction Day, Sadie Hawkins Day, Sweden: All Saints' Day, United Nations: International Day to End Impunity for Crimes Against Journalists
3. Canada: New Inuit Territory Approved (1992), *Cliché Day, Dewey Day, Daylight Saving Time Ends, Dominica: National Day, *Japan: Culture Day, Micronesia and Panama: Independence Day, Public Television Day, *Sandwich Day, SOS Day, Zero Tasking Day

4. Australia: Recreation Day, Fill Our Staplers Day, Italy: Victory Day, *King Tut Tomb Discovery (1922), Mischief Night, *National Chicken Lady Day, National Easy Bake Oven Day, National Traffic Professionals Day, Panama: Flag Day, Russia: Unity Day, UNESCO Day, *Will Rogers (1879)
5. El Salvador: Day of the First Shout for Independence, *England: Guy Fawkes Day, Firewood Day, General Election Day, Israel: Aliyah Day (Yom Ha'Aliyah), *Roy Rogers (1911), *Shattered Backboard Day, United Nations: World Tsunami Awareness Day, Vivian Leigh–Scarlett O'Hara Day (1913)
6. National Block It Out Day, Saxophone Day, *United Nations: International Day for Preventing the Exploitation of the Environment in War and Armed Conflict
7. Bangladesh: Solidarity Day, Madam Curie Day, First Black Governor Elected (1989), National Men Make Dinner Day, Republican Symbol (1874), Return Day, Russia: Revolution Day
8. Abet and Aid Punsters Day, Cook Something Bold and Pungent Day, Shakespeare Authorship Mystery Day, *X–ray Day
9. *Berlin Wall Opened (1989), Boston Fire (1872), Cambodia: Independence Day, East Coast Blackout (1965), Germany: Kristallnacht, National Child Safety Council Day
10. *Area Code Day (1951), Claude Rains Day, Marine Corps Day, Panama: First Shout of Independence, Sesame Street Anniversary (50th, 1969)
11. Angola: Independence Day, *Bonza Bottler Day™, Canada: Remembrance Day, China: Singles Day, Columbia: Cartagena: Independence Day, Death/Duty Day, England: Remembrance Day, God Bless America Day, Japan: Origami Day, Maldives: Republic Day, Martinmas, Poland: Independence Day, Sweden: Saint Martin's Day, Switzerland: Martinmas Goose (Martinigians), Veterans Day (100th Anniversary, (1919)
12. India: Guru Nanak's Birth, Mexico: Postman's Day, Sun Yat-Sen (traditional), World Pneumonia Day
13. Holland Tunnel Day, Japan: Shichi–Go–San (Seven-Five-Three) Day
14. Dow Jones Tops 1,000 (1642), Guinea-Bissau: Readjustment Movement's Day, India: Children's Day, Loosen Up Lighten Up Day, Moby Dick Day, Claude Monet Day, *United Nations: World Diabetes Day
15. *America Recycles Day, Belgium: Dynasty Day, Brazil: Republic Day, George Spelvin Day, *National Bundt (Pan) Day
16. Estonia: Day of National Rebirth, *Lewis and Clark Expedition Reaches Pacific Ocean (1805), PCS Day, Saint Eustatius, Thailand: Elephant Roundup at Surin, *United Nations: International Day for Tolerance
17. Germany: Volkstrauertag, *Homemade Bread Day, National Unfriend Day, Suez Canal Day, United Nations: World Day of Remembrance for Road Traffic Victims, World Prematurity Day
18. Haiti: Army Day, Latvia: Independence Day, *Married to a Scorpio Support Day, *Mickey Mouse's Birthday (1928), Oman: National Holiday
19. Belize: Garifuna Day, Cold War Ends (1990), *Dedication Day (1862), First Automatic Toll Collection Machine (65th Anniversary, 1954), Gandhi Day, Garfield Day, *"Have A Bad Day" Day, Monaco: National Holiday, Puerto Rico: Discovery Day, United Nations: World Toilet Day
20. *Bill of Rights Day, Edwin Powell Hubble Day, Germany: Buss Und Bettag, *Mandelbrot Day (1924), Mexico: Revolution Day, *Name Your PC Day, National Educational

Support Professionals Day, Transgender Day of Remembrance, *United Nations: African Industrialization Day, United Nations: Universal Children's Day
21. Dow Jones Tops 5,000, Great American Smoke-out (third Thursday), *Sir Samuel Cunard (1787), *United Nations: World Television Day, World Hello Day, World Philosophy Day
22. Charles De Gaulle Day 1890), Edward Teach "Blackbeard" Death, (1718), *George Eliot (1819), Humane Society of the US Day (1954), Lebanon: Independence Day, Substitute Educators Day
23. Alascattalo Day (About Alaska and humor), Billy the Kid Day, Fibonacci Day, Boris Karloff Day, Fibonacci Day, Harpo Marx Day, International Aura Awareness Day, Japan: Labor Thanksgiving Day
24. Brownielocks and Brunette Pride Day, *Celebrate Your Unique Talent Day, *Dale Carnegie (1888), *D.B. Cooper Day, Germany: Totensonntag, Stir Up Sunday,
25. *Andrew Carnegie (1835), Bosnia and Herzegovina: National Day, *JFK Day (1960), Saint Catherine's Day, Suriname: Independence Day, Switzerland: Zibelemarit (Onion Market), United Nations: International Day for the Elimination of Violence Against Women Day
26. Charles Schultz (1922), Mongolia: Republic Day
27. Bruce Lee Day, Face Transplant Day, Israel: Sigd, Laerdal Tunnel Opening (2000), Spitesgiving, Tie One On Day™
28. *Albania: Independence Day (1912), Chad: Republic Day, *Lévi–Strauss (1908), Mauritania: Independence Day, Panama: Independence from Spain, Thanksgiving Day
29. Alcott Day, *CS Lewis (1898), Black Friday, Buy Nothing Day (20–30), Dine Over Your Kitchen Sink Day, *Electronic Greetings Day, Family Day in Nevada, National Flossing Day, Native American Heritage Day, *United Nations: International Day of Solidarity with the Palestinian People
30. Articles of Peace Between Great Britain and the US (1782), Barbados: Independence Day, Computer Security Day, Saint Andrew's Day, Small Business Saturday, *Stay Home Because You're Well Day, United Nations: Day of Remembrance for all Victims of Chemical Warfare

HOLIDAY MARKETING IDEAS FOR NOVEMBER

Picture Book Month —Christmas is just around the corner and it is picture book time. So, you are sure to want to take advantage of marketing if you are a picture book author. If you are not, then you might consider running a contest and give away a set of picture books as the prize.

Perhaps you are an editor, designer, or other publishing professional, now is the perfect time to showcase your talents and abilities. For the rest of us, celebrate with lines from your favorite picture books posted on social media, cards, notes, and graphics.

Nov 1 Hockey Mask Day—This weird and wacky holiday is all about protecting ourselves which is something we all need to do. Therefore, business owners who are financial advisors, insurance, attorneys, doctors, nurses, and even skin care consultants and fitness or health advocates all could make this a really good day to market their wares. Seminars, webinars, chats, or hangouts all are appropriate venues to host your event.

For those who want to do something easier but still get the attention of your fans you could host a hockey mask design contest like Canada held in 2015. You can use their template which I have duplicated and placed in the Samples appendix, but be sure to brand it to your business, of course.

Lastly, you have tips, tweets, and social media to contend with for those who don't have the time or fortitude to take on the big challenge of an event.

Nov 4 National Traffic Professionals Day—Do you have crossing guards in your area? We have several schools near our home in Florida. They tirelessly guide our children across the busy roadways to safety on the opposite side of the street. Thus, a terrific way to celebrate this holiday and garner the media's attention is to get together a group of either employees or business people, maybe even an artist or two, and put together bags or baskets of goodies with a thank you note from your company(s) included. Then on this weird and wacky holiday go around and hand them out to the traffic professionals in your area. If you let the media know what you are doing, I can almost guarantee they'll notice and want to cover your event.

Another idea is to focus on the aspects of their service and create an event that's theme is properly related. Themes that might work could be health and safety, moving in a positive direction with your life and business, or even creating a business plan. I am sure you can come up with a few of your own if you take a moment to ponder.

Nov 10 Area Code Day—Today's weird and wacky holiday is about organization and making our lives easier to get where we want and need to go. As you reflect on how to celebrate while marketing your business keep those thoughts in mind. For fun you could create a map and have your friends and colleagues, business partners and clients put a pin in the map where their area code belongs and write their name or business and area code in the attached pin text box.

Besides events, you always have the option of merely posting social media graphics or sending out notes to your customers/clients. You'll find a graphic you can use in the Sample appendix or create your own.

Nov 14 Loosen Up Lighten Up Day—Note to self: Loosen Up; Lighten Up! It's time to unwind. Destress your life and find solace. When you are at peace with your inner core you are better able to face the challenges that are around the bend. So, take the time today to show others how to decompress through exercise, prayer, meditation, aroma therapy, proper diet, or whatever it takes. Use the tools at your disposal to share advice or tips and techniques and you may find yourself feeling less stressful in the process.

Take a group for a walk in the woods or on the beach, join a yoga class, or spend some time doing something artistic like painting or crafting. There are several ways to gather as a group and help them destress without inundating them with words in a seminar or webinar.

If you can't think of anything else, you can always just tweet or post social media images and messages. However, if this is your business, then you have the chance to show how much of an expert you are by sharing tips and techniques to unwind on Loosen Up Lighten Up Day. You'll find a graphic for both males and females in the Samples appendix that you can customize and use for your marketing purposes.

*Note: This was so good I couldn't resist using it again this year, but with a few new suggestions. This just goes to prove there is more than one way to celebrate any weird and wacky holiday.

Nov 20 Name Your PC Day — Why not? And this isn't just for PC's. Mac users can join the fun too. Will you go outlandish or run of the mill? This is one we featured in 2017. If you are lucky enough to own that edition you already have a flyer that celebrates this weird and wacky holiday. That flyer explains how to change your computer's name on both Macs and Windows devices. Yes, you really can officially change the name of your computer. Ginger's Home Computer is just, well, lame!

Besides giving out cards that explain the process that are branded to your business don't forget you always have the option to host a fun Name Your PC Day event. This you can even do online. Help each other decide on just the perfect name or share how you came up with yours.

In the Samples appendix you will find two social media sized graphics for your use.

DECEMBER

MONTH-LONG HOLIDAYS

Dec 1 – Jan 6 Netherlands: Midwinter Horn Blowing
Dec 14 – 28 Halcyon Days
Dec 14 – Jan 5, 2019 Christmas Bird Count
Dec 17 – Feb 2, 2019 Take a New Year's Resolution to Stop Smoking (TANYRSS)

Bingo's Birthday Month, National Impaired Driving Prevention Month, National Write a Business Plan Month, Safe Toys and Gifts Month, Worldwide Food Service Safety Month

WEEK-LONG HOLIDAYS

Dec 1 – 6 Radiological Society of North America Scientific
Dec 1 – 7 Cookie Exchange Week
Dec 2 – 6 National Older Driver Safety Awareness Week
Dec 3 – 10 Clerc-Gallaudet Week,
Dec 5 – 7 Holly Jolly Weekend
Dec 10 – 17 Human Rights Week
Dec 17 – 23 Saturnalia
Dec 19 – 31 Christmastide in Virginia
Dec 23 – 30 Chanukah
Dec 26 – Jan 1, 2017 Kwanzaa

DAILY HOLIDAYS

1. Advent (First Sunday), Antarctica Day, *Basketball Day, *Bifocals at the Monitor Liberation Day, Canada: Yukon Oeder of Pioneeers (125th Anniversary, 1894), Christmas to Remember, *Civil Air Patrol Day, Handel's Messiah Sing-Along, Portugal: Independence Day, Romania: National Holiday, Rosa Parks Day, *United Nations: World AIDS Day
2. *Artificial Heart Transplant Day (1967), Central African Republic: National Day Observed, Cider Monday, Cyber Monday, England: Walter Plinge Day, Laos: National Day, *Joseph Bell (1837), National Mutt Day — December, *Special Education Day, United Arab Emirates: Independence Day, *United Nations: International Day for the Abolition of Slavery Day
3. First Heart Transplant (1967), Giving Tuesday, *United Nations: International Day of Persons with Disabilities
4. Mary Celeste Discovery Day, National Grange Day, Saint Barbara's Day, *Samuel Butler (1835), Special Kids Day
5. *AFL–CIO Founded (1955), Austria: Krampuslauf, *Bathtub Party Day, Haiti: Discovery Day, "Irrational Exuberance" Day, Montgomery Bus Boycott Remembrance Day, National

Christmas Tree Lighting (tentative), *United Nations: International Volunteer Day for Economic and Social Development, United Nations: World Soil Day, *Walt Disney (1901)

6. Ecuador: Day of Quito: Founding (1534), Finland: Independence Day, Ghana: National Farmers' Day, Missouri Earthquakes (1811), *National Miners' Day, *National Pawnbrokers Day, National Sales Person's Day, *Saint Nicholas Day, Spain: Constitution Day
7. Armenian Earthquake (1988), Bike Shop Day, Cote D'Ivoire: Commemoration Day, Iran: Students Day, *National Fire Safety Council Day (1979), *National Pearl Harbor Remembrance Day, *United Nations: International Civil Aviation Day
8. *Eli Whitney (1765), Feast of Immaculate Conception, Guam: Lady of Camarin Day, Intermediate-Range Nuclear Forces Treaty (INF) Signed (1987), NAFTA Day, National Lard Day, Soviet Union Dissolved (1991), Uzbekistan: Constitution Day
9. Tanzania: Independence and Republic Day, *United Nations: International Anti-Corruption Day, United Nations: International Day of Commemoration and Dignity of the victims of the Crime of Genocide and of the Prevention of this Crime
10. *Ada Lovelace (1815), *Dewey Decimal System Day, *Emily Dickinson (1830), Encyclopedia Britannica First Published (1879), *Human Rights Day, James Addams Day, *Nobel Prize Awards Ceremonies, *Thomas Hopkins Gallaudet (1787), Thailand: Constitution Day, *United Nations: Human Rights Day
11. Burkino Faso: Independence Day, Kaleidoscope Day, *UNICEF Birthday, *United Nations: International Mountain Day
12. *Bonza Bottler Day™, Day of Our Lady of Guadalupe, Kenya: Jamhuri Day (Independence Day), Mexico: Guadalupe Day, *Poinsettia Day, *Puerto Rico: Las Mañanitas, Turkmenistan: Neutrality Day, United Nations: International Day of Neutrality
13. Malta: Republic Day, *New Zealand Discovery (1642), Official Lost and Found Day, Sweden: Saint Lucia Day
14. *Doolittle Day, Gingerbread Decorating Day, National Day of the Horse, Nostradamus (1503), South Pole Discovery (1911)
15. *Bill of Rights Day, *Cat Herders Day, Curaçao: Kingdom Day and Antillean Flag Day, Puerto Rico: Navidades
16. Bahrain: Independence Day, Bangladesh: Victory Day, *Barbie and Barney Backlash Day, Boston Tea Party Day, Calabria Earthquake (1857), *Jane Austen (1775), Kazakhstan: Independence Day, *Ludwig Van Beethoven (1770), Mexico: Posadas, Philippines; Philippine Christmas Observance and Simbang Gabi, South Africa: Reconciliation Day, *United Nations: Zionism Day
17. *Azteck Calendar Stone Discovery Day (1790), *Clean Air Day, First Flight Anniversary Celebration Day, *Joseph Henry (1797), *Wright Brothers Day
18. *Benjamin O Davis, Jr. (1912), *Joseph Grimaldi (1778), Mexico: Feast of Our Lady of Solitude, Niger: Republic Day, "To Tell the Truth" Day, United Nations: Arabic Language Day, *United Nations: International Migrants Day
19. Titanic Day
20. Montgomery Bus Boycott Ends (1956), *Mudd Day, Underdog Day, *United Nations: International Human Solidarity Day
21. Celebrate Short Fiction Day, Benjamin Disraeli Birth (1804), *Crossword Puzzle Day, *Forefathers Day, *Heinrich Böll (1917), *Humbug Day, *Phileas Fogg Win a Wager Day, Pilgrim Landing, Yalda, Yule
22. Be a Lover of Silence Day, Chanukah (begins at sundown), First Gorilla Born in Captivity (1956), *Giacomo Puccini (1858), Oglethorpe Day

23. *Federal Reserve System (1913), Festivus Day, First Non-stop Flight Around the World (1987), Metric Conversion Act (1975), *Transistor Day (1947)
24. Austria: "Silent Night, Holy Night", *Christmas Eve, First Surface-to-Surface Guided Missile, *James Prescott Joule (1818), Libya: Independence Day
25. *A'Phabet Day or No-L-Day, *Christmas Day, Cuba: Christmas Returns, *Clara Barton (1821), Taiwan: Constitution Day, Washington Crosses the Delaware (1776)
26. *Bahamas: Junkanoo, Boxing Day, Ireland: Day of the Wren, Luxembourg: Blessing of the Wine, National Candy Cane Day, *National Whiner's Day, Radium Discovery Day, Saint Stephen's Day, Second Day of Christmas, Slovenia: Independence Day, South Africa: Day of Goodwill, *United Kingdom: Boxing Day
27. "Howdy Doody" Day, *Johannes Kepler (1571), *Louis Pasteur (1822), Saint John Feast Day
28. Australia: Proclamation Day, *Cinema Day, Endangered Species Day, *Holy Innocents Day or Childermas, *Pledge of Allegiance Day
29. Andrew Johnson Wreath-Laying, Saint Thomas of Canterbury: Feast Day, *Tick Tock Day, *YMCA Day
30. *Falling Needles Family Fest Day, *Rudyard Kipling (1865), "Let's Make a Deal" Day, Philippines: Rizal Day, USSR DAY (1922)
31. *First Nights, First US Bank Opens (1781), *Japan: Namahage, *Leap Second Adjustment Time Day, *Make Up Your Mind Day, *New Year's Eve, No Interruptions Day, Saint Sylvester's Day, Scotland: Hogmany

HOLIDAY MARKETING IDEAS FOR DECEMBER

Safe Toys and Gifts Month—Soon it will be gift giving time. This month we feature safe toys and gifts. If you sell anything, there's no reason not to highlight your business and wares this month in your marketing. What could be more safe than coaching services, services of any kind would be ideal; doctor, nurse, coach, business services, message, you name it, the sky's the limit. Of course, physical products are what the name implies, but don't think you can't benefit if you don't have a physical product to sell.

Think cross-promotion selling. Spend the month talking about the benefits of using someone else's offering(s) and how they can impact your audience's lives. The reason I suggest cross-promotion is that it's easier to talk about the best restaurant in town than it is to talk about your own. And, it will be more easily accepted as fact, something we all need to make a buying decision.

If you insist on going it alone and promoting your own products and services, put together graphics that showcase the benefits of the offering, notice I didn't say 'features'. Then share them on your social media channels for highest impact. Advertisements are great for this marketing push, try Google, Facebook, or even Amazon for starters. And, don't forget, people still do read newspapers and listen to the radio. If you can afford to advertise in these places, you'll be a leg up on your competition.

Dec 2 United Nations: International Day for the Abolition of Slavery Day—Today we recognize the abhorrent practice of slavery. We are all victims of it. You're either another person's slave or your own. Sometimes it's a necessary evil, others a joy. Yes, slavery can be a joy when you are working towards a sought-after goal. Seeing the progress as you accomplish the small feats, can give you great satisfaction.

When hosting seminars/webinars today focus on freedom from the things that plague you and your customers and clients. Fear is the number one world's greatest taskmaster. So, overcoming fear could be a big part of your marketing effort or event. Tips and techniques can be shared as well. You need not host an event, but truth be told, events do increase your reach and thus your bottom line.

Of course, fear is just one slave master. There are numerous others to be considered. Time is another one. If you have trouble with time management, don't feel alone. Others also suffer from this horrendous beast. Time management tips and advice posted on social media or an event that includes this topic would do well today. I'm sure you can come up with a few others too.

You'll find an event poster in the making in the Samples appendix. As always, feel free to modify it to meet your brand and needs.

Dec 7 National Fire Safety Council Day — Fire is beautiful when it is controlled, e.g., in the fireplace on a chilly winter morn. But, when it rages out of control, i.e., in a forest fire, well, that's another matter altogether! Today, in your marketing efforts focus on the controlled burn of keeping your businesses on track. Don't attempt to do everything at once. Rather, map out a plan for your business that you can reasonably adhere to next year and begin implementing it. When it gets out of control, reevaluate and adjust as the winds of time blow.

If you are up to the task, an event that helps other business owners see the potential in their businesses and develop a plan would be a superbly satisfying way to spend today. Help them beat down the flames of temptation to jump on the next best thing raging around them. They will thank you in the end. See the Samples appendix for a graphic you can use to share.

Dec 8 National Lard Day — We all know what lard is, it is fat in its truest form. Today is the day to get the lard out. Get it out of your business, your body, and your life. So, you could focus on any of these aspects. If you own a health or fitness business (cooking and food businesses are just too obvious to fail to mention) the solution to marketing your business today is obvious. However, most of us would do better from focusing on getting the lard out of our businesses. Share tips on how to remove the lard that is greasing over your profits, or how about the fat that is covering your success. When you share your tips and advice on better managing a business, they are always welcome.

Dec 23 Festivus Day — This tongue-in-cheek secular holiday involving a plain aluminum pole, an airing of grievances, and wrestling tells me that your focus today would do well to share means and measure for customer service or conflict resolution. Whether you are a therapist or a business owner, we all experience times of conflict. Plan your day around sharing sage advice, be it in a live event or timely quotes. You'll find a few quotes and a graphic you can use in the Sample appendix. But, don't stop there. A quick search will provide a plethora of information that you can share. A fine book to read, share, or even offer as a prize is Robert Lucas' book, *Customer Service Skills for Success*. Look for it in the Resources.

Appendix A: SAMPLES

Sample Press Release

FOR IMMEDIATE RELEASE
30+ YEAR LOCAL VETERAN BUSINESS OWNER / AUTHOR PARTNERS WITH PNC BANK
CLEARWATER, FL — SEPTEMBER 21, 2014

Local author and publisher, Ginger Marks, partners with Clearwater's PNC Bank to provide insight and advice for prospective, new, and experienced business owners. Ginger will be available to chat and sign copies of her award-winning book, Complete Library of Entrepreneurial Wisdom, and PNC Financial experts will be on hand to field your questions and educate you on business financial matters.

Mrs. Marks has spent 30+ years in the Tampa Bay area honing her skill as an entrepreneur. Having owned and operated multiple businesses, including a restaurant and a multimillion-dollar surgical clinic, she knows her way around business and how to operate one successfully.

Mrs. Marks states, "Owning a business takes many talents and the determination to succeed. In the course of my business operations I have experienced both the ups and the downs of the financial market. Without the knowledge of how to structure your finances to support your dreams you endanger your success. This is why I have partnered with PNC with the release of this important work."

Event date and location: October 9, 2014 between 5:30 and 6:30 pm at 2498 Gulf-to-Bay Blvd. Books available at your local bookstore and at this event.
# # #
MEDIA CONTACT: Ginger Marks, ginger.marks@documeantdesings.com 1–727–565–8500.

Pop Music Day Artist/Song Titles

Use these artist or song titles to create some fun games. There are many, many more. This is just to get you started. A line from the song will work for a cryptogram with extra points for naming either the artist or song title.

A-Ha: Take On Me

Chicago: 25 or 6 to 4

John Lennon: Imagine

Lena Horn: Stormy Weather

Judy Garland: Over the Rainbow

Everly Brothers: Bye-bye Love

Jeff Buckley: Hallelujah

USA for Africa: We Are the World

Electric Light Orchestra: Mr. Blue Sky

Queen: Bohemian Rhapsody

Beach Boys: Good Vibrations

The Band: The Weight

Joni Mitchell: Big Yellow Taxi

Elton John: Your Song

Bobby Darin: Mack the Knife

Bruce Springsteen: Born to Run

Janet Jackson: Escapade

U2: One

Madonna: Like a Prayer

Aba: Dancing Queen

Tina Turner: Proud Mary

Village People: Macho Man

Simon and Garfunkel: Bridge Over Troubled Water

Beatles: Yesterday

Judy Collins: Send in the Clowns

Don McLean: American Pie

Celine Dion: My Heart Will Go On

Rolling Stones: (I Can't Get No) Satisfaction

Christina Aguilera: Beautiful

Celine Dion & Josh Groban: The Prayer

Righteous Brothers: Unchained Melody

Carly Simon: Your So Vain

Beatles: Hey Jude

The Doors: Light My Fire

Sam Cooke: You Send Me

Whitney Houston: I Will Always Love You

Bee Gees: You Should Be Dancing

Otis Redding: (Sittin' On) The Dock of the Bay

Aretha Franklin: Respect

Elvis Presley: Heartbreak Hotel

Prince and the Revolution: When Doves Cry

Pop Music Song Cryptograms

__ __ __y, I __'__ __ __ __ __ __, __y __ __ __ __ __

BODY, IT'S SO HOT, MY BODY (Macho Man)

__a__ __ __ __ __ __ f__ __ __ __ __ __ __ __ __a__ __
f __ a __

WAITING FOR THE BREAK OF DAY (25 or 6 to 4)

M__ __ __ __ __ M__v__ __ __ __ M__ __ __
__ __ __ __

MY BABY MOVES AT MIDNIGHT (You Should be Dancing)

__ __ __i__ __ __ I __ __ __ __ __ __ __ __ I __ w__ __ I
__ __ __ __ __ __ __ __i__ __

AT FIRST I THOUGHT IT WAS INFATUATION
(You Send Me)

__ __ __d __ __ __ __a__ __ __ __ __e a__ __
__ __ __e

FIND OUT WHAT IT MEANS TO ME (Respect)

__ __b__ __ I'__ __ __ __ __ __i__ __ __ __ __ __
__ __ __ r

MAYBE I'M JUST LIKE MY FATHER (When Doves Cry)

Name This Artist

For an added bit of fun time the contestants for best time to solve. That way you can play this game all day online if you choose.

Answers:

1. Prince	2. Celine Dion	3. Paul Simon
4. Otis Redding	5. Bruce Springsteen	6. Billy Joel
7. Madonna	8. Tito Jackson	9. Robin Gibbs

Podcast Directory

Between the Covers (Author Interviews) — https://www.stitcher.com/podcast/between-the-covers

Entrepreneur On Fire — https://www.stitcher.com/podcast/entrepreneur-on-fire-tim-ferriss-other-incredible-entrepreneurs/

Food Heals — https://www.stitcher.com/podcast/allison-melody/the-food-heals-podcast

Foundr Magazine Podcast — https://www.stitcher.com/podcast/nathan-chan-online-entrepreneur-magazine-publisher-technolog

Nutrition Diva — https://www.stitcher.com/podcast/the-nutrition-divas-quick-and-dirty-tips-for-eating-well-and

Real Fast Results, with Daniel Hall — http://realfastresults.com

The EntreprenHer Show — http://www.TheEntreprenHerShow.com

The Savvy Psychologist's Quick and Dirty Tips for Better Mental Health — https://www.stitcher.com/podcast/savvy-psychologist

The Small Business Big Marketing Show — https://www.stitcher.com/podcast/small-business-big-marketing

The Ultimate Health Podcast — https://www.stitcher.com/podcast/the-ultimate-health-podcast

Like A Boss: Insights with Entrepreneurial Insiders, Helping You Rise To the Top, with Heather Ann Havenwood — www.HeatherHavenwood.com/podcast

Judgment Day Card

Customize any of the designs in this book with your business name and URL. Need help? Contact Ginger for assistance.

Note: If you would like any of the full-size images provided in this book please email Ginger at designer@documeantdesigns.com.

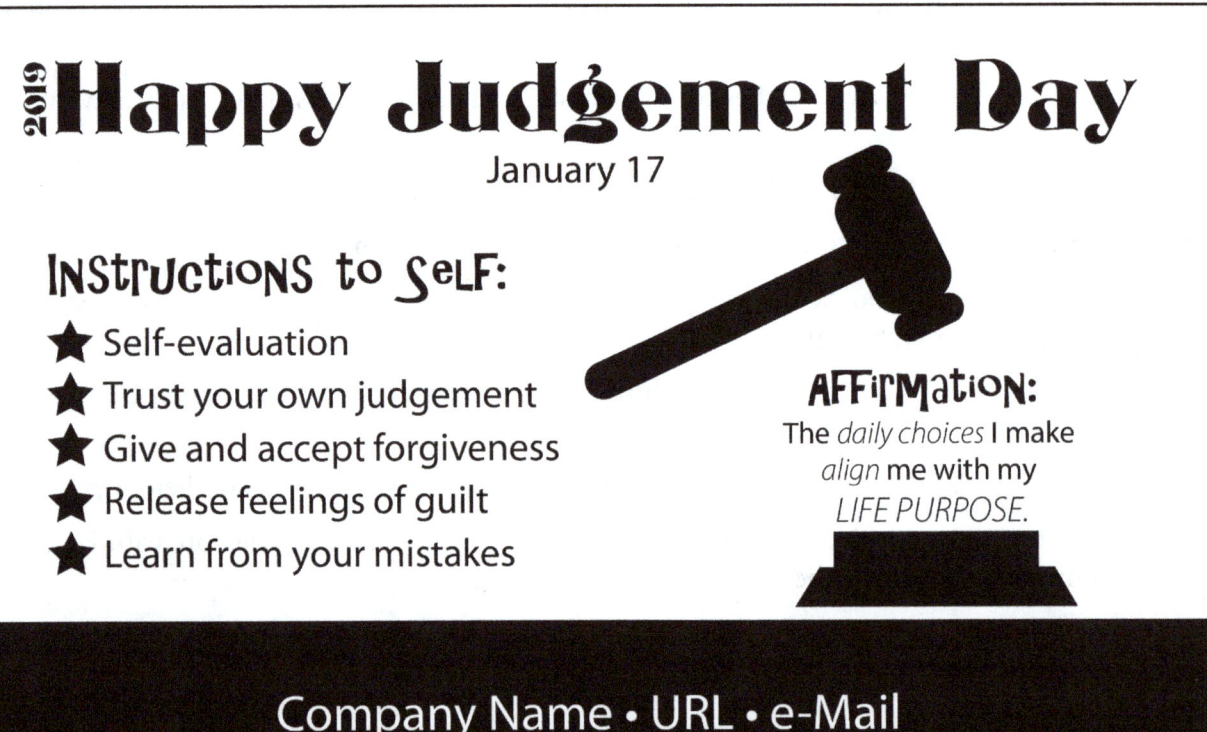

Croissant Day Recipes

French Croissant

1 Tbsp yeast

1 cup warm water

1tsp sugar

3/4 cup milk

1/3 cup sugar

1-1/2 tsp salt

1 egg

1-1/2 cups flour

1/4 cup cooking oil

4 cups flour

1/2 pound butter

Directions

Mix yeast, warm water and sugar in the bottom of a mixing bowl. After the yeast starts to work, add the milk, sugar, salt, egg and 1-1/2 cups flour. Mix together until the mixture is smooth. Set aside.

Cut the butter into the 4 cups flour until the butter is the size of peas.

Pour the wet batter over the flour/butter mix and stir together until combined. Do not overmix. Cover the dough and put in the refrigerator for several hours. The dough will keep well for several days.

When ready to bake, divide the cold dough into four sections, removing one section. Return the other three sections to the refrigerator until ready to use. Form the 1/4 dough into a ball and roll it out into a circle about 1/2 inch thick. Cut the dough into four sections. Starting at the wide end, roll the section up until the tip is over the roll and bend the ends to form the crescent shape. Place on a baking sheet. Continue with the rest of the sections.

The dough can be made into smaller rolls by cutting into more sections.

Let the rolls rise for an hour, covered with a damp towel or plastic wrap, until twice their original size.

Uncover rolls, place in a COLD oven at 325 degrees for 18 minutes or until brown. Cool on racks.

Classic Croissant Sandwich
Makes 1

1 croissant
1 slice cheese
1/3 can tuna or salmon, drained
sausage slices
Mayonnaise

Directions
Cut the croissant in half horizontally.

Open the tuna (Chunk White Albacore tuna or salmon in water) add mayonnaise (however amount you want, but if you add too much, it will get watery) and mix it together with a spoon. This will be the base of your sandwich.

Fry your eggs well done and while you are frying your eggs, if you decide to add sausages, cook those on the skillet too.

Place your cheese (any kind is okay) on top of your tuna base and on top of your cheese, add your fried eggs and then top it with your sausages. Then close the sandwich with the other half of your croissant.

Dark Chocolate Croissant Bread Pudding

8 croissants, torn into 2-inch pieces
1 cup semisweet chocolate chunks
8 large eggs
1 cup sugar
1 tablespoon grated orange zest
1-1/2 teaspoons ground cinnamon
1/4 teaspoon ground nutmeg
1/8 teaspoon salt
3 cups 2% milk
1 cup orange juice
2 teaspoons vanilla extract

Directions
Preheat oven to 350°. Place croissants in a greased 13x9-in. baking dish; sprinkle with chocolate chunks. In a large bowl, whisk eggs, sugar, orange zest, cinnamon, nutmeg and salt until blended. Stir in milk, orange juice and vanilla; pour over top. Let stand about 15 minutes or until bread is softened.

Bake, uncovered, 40-45 minutes or until puffed and golden brown; cover loosely with foil during last 10 minutes if top browns too quickly. Serve warm.

Chicken Salad Croissant Sandwiches
Serves 4

This is one of my very favorite ways to eat croissants, if you don't count chocolate croissants. *wink*

2 cups shredded cooked chicken breast
1 cup seedless red grapes, halved
1/2 cup chopped cashews
1 celery rib, chopped
1/3 cup grated Parmesan cheese
1 green onion, chopped
1/2 cup mayonnaise
1/3 cup buttermilk
2 teaspoons lemon juice
1 teaspoon dill weed
1 teaspoon dried parsley flakes
1/4 teaspoon salt
1/4 teaspoon garlic powder
1/4 teaspoon pepper
4 croissants, split

Directions
In a small bowl, combine the first six ingredients. In another bowl, whisk mayonnaise, buttermilk, lemon juice and seasonings. Pour over chicken mixture; mix well. Spoon chicken salad onto croissant bottoms. Replace tops.

Croissant Breakfast Casserole
1 jar (18 ounces) orange marmalade
1/2 cup apricot preserves
1/3 cup orange juice
3 teaspoons grated orange zest
6 croissants, split
5 large eggs
1 cup half-and-half cream
1 teaspoon almond or vanilla extract
Quartered fresh strawberries

Directions
In a small bowl, mix marmalade, preserves, orange juice and zest. Arrange croissant bottoms in a greased 13x9-in. baking dish. Spread with 1-1/2 cups marmalade mixture. Add croissant tops.

In another bowl, whisk eggs, cream and extract; pour over croissants. Spoon remaining marmalade mixture over tops. Refrigerate, covered, overnight.

Preheat oven to 350°. Remove casserole from refrigerator while oven heats. Bake, uncovered, 25-30 minutes or until a knife inserted in the center comes out clean. Let stand 5 minutes before serving. Serve with strawberries.

Croissant Pudding with Chocolate Kahlua Sauce

6 croissants, torn into pieces
4 large egg yolks
2 large eggs
3 cups heavy whipping cream
2-1/4 cups sugar
1-1/2 cups half-and-half cream
4-1/2 teaspoons vanilla extract
1-1/2 teaspoons salt

Sauce:
2 ounces unsweetened chocolate, coarsely chopped
2 tablespoons butter
1 cup sugar
1/2 cup evaporated milk
Dash salt
3 tablespoons Kahlua (coffee liqueur)
6 croissants, torn into pieces
4 large egg yolks
2 large eggs
3 cups heavy whipping cream
2-1/4 cups sugar
1-1/2 cups half-and-half cream
4-1/2 teaspoons vanilla extract
1-1/2 teaspoons salt

Directions
Divide croissant pieces among nine greased 10-oz. ramekins or custard cups. Place on baking sheets.

In a large bowl, combine the egg yolks, eggs, cream, sugar, half-and-half, vanilla and salt. Pour over croissant pieces; let stand for 15 minutes or until croissants are softened. Bake at 325° for 40–45 minutes or until a knife inserted in the center comes out clean.

For sauce, in a small saucepan, melt chocolate and butter over medium-low heat. Add the sugar, milk and salt; cook and stir for 3–4 minutes or until thickened. Remove from the heat; stir in Kahlua. Serve with warm pudding.

New England Bean & Bog Cassoulet

5 tablespoons olive oil, divided
8 boneless skinless chicken thighs (about 2 pounds)
1 package (12 ounces) fully cooked Italian chicken sausage links, cut into 1/2-in. slices
4 shallots, finely chopped
2 teaspoons minced fresh rosemary or 1/2 teaspoon dried rosemary, crushed
2 teaspoons minced fresh thyme or 1/2 teaspoon dried thyme
1 can (28 ounces) fire-roasted diced tomatoes, undrained

1 can (16 ounces) baked beans
1 cup chicken broth
1/2 cup fresh or frozen cranberries
3 day-old croissants, cubed (about 6 cups)
1/2 teaspoon lemon-pepper seasoning
2 tablespoons minced fresh parsley

Directions

Preheat oven to 400°. In a Dutch oven, heat 2 tablespoons oil over medium heat. In batches, brown chicken thighs on both sides; remove from pan, reserving drippings. Add sausage; cook and stir until lightly browned. Remove from pan.

In same pan, heat 1 tablespoon oil over medium heat. Add shallots, rosemary and thyme; cook and stir until shallots are tender, 1-2 minutes. Stir in tomatoes, beans, broth and cranberries. Return chicken and sausage to pan; bring to a boil. Bake, covered, until chicken is tender, 20-25 minutes.

Toss croissant pieces with remaining oil; sprinkle with lemon pepper. Arrange over chicken mixture. Bake, uncovered, until croissants are golden brown, 12-15 minutes. Sprinkle with parsley.

Taco Crescent Ring

1 pound ground beef
1 pkg (1 oz) Old El Paso™ taco seasoning mix
½ cup water
1 cup shredded Cheddar cheese (4 oz)
2 cans (8 oz each) Pillsbury™ refrigerated crescent dinner rolls
Shredded lettuce, chopped tomatoes, sliced ripe olives, taco sauce or salsa, as desired

Directions

Heat oven to 375°F. In 10-inch nonstick skillet, cook beef until no longer pink. Add taco seasoning mix and 1/2 cup water. Simmer 3 to 4 minutes or until slightly thickened. In medium bowl, mix beef mixture and cheese.

Unroll both cans of dough; separate into 16 triangles. On ungreased large cookie sheet, arrange triangles in ring so short sides of triangles form a 5-inch circle in center. Dough will overlap. Dough ring should look like the sun.

Spoon beef mixture on the half of each triangle closest to center of ring.

Bring each dough triangle up over filling, tucking dough under bottom layer of dough to secure it. Repeat around ring until entire filling is enclosed (some filling might show a little).

Buffalo Chicken Crescent Ring

4 oz cream cheese (half of 8-oz package), softened
1/4 cup hot sauce or red pepper sauce
2-1/2 cups chopped cooked chicken (1/2-inch pieces)
1 cup shredded Monterey Jack cheese (4 oz)
2 cans (8 oz each) Pillsbury™ refrigerated crescent rolls
1/3 cup crumbled blue cheese

Directions

Heat oven to 375°F. In small bowl, mix cream cheese and hot sauce until smooth. Mix in chicken and shredded cheese just until combined.

Unroll both cans of dough; separate into 16 triangles. On ungreased large cookie sheet, arrange triangles in ring so short sides of triangles form a 5-inch circle in center. Dough will overlap. Dough ring should look like a sun.

Spoon cream cheese mixture on the half of each triangle closest to center of ring. Top with blue cheese crumbles.

Bring each dough triangle up over filling, tucking dough under bottom layer of dough to secure it. Repeat around ring until entire filling is enclosed (some filling might show a little).

Bake 20 to 25 minutes or until dough is golden brown and thoroughly baked. Cool 5 to 10 minutes before cutting into serving slices.

Easy, 20 Minute Chocolate Croissants Recipe

Makes 8

1 8-oz can refrigerated crescent rolls
1 cup semisweet chocolate chips
1 large egg, beaten
1 teaspoon coconut oil or butter (optional)

Directions

Preheat the oven to 350 degrees Fahrenheit (176 degrees Celsius). Line a sheet tray with parchment paper or a silicon baking mat.

Open the can of crescent rolls and separate the dough into the pre-cut triangles, placing them onto the lined sheet tray.

Arrange about 1 tablespoon* of the semisweet chocolate chips close in the center of each of the triangles of crescent dough.

Roll the croissant dough according to the instructions on the can, starting from the wide end and rolling to the opposite point. After rolling, curve the dough to make them into a croissant shape.

Brush the croissants lightly with the beaten egg, making sure to apply a small amount under the pointed tip of the dough. Lightly press down as you do so in order to ensure that the tip of the dough stays put and help to give the finished croissants that golden glow.

Bake for 13 to 16 minutes, or until the dough is a deep golden brown.

Remove the croissants from the baking sheet and allow to cool for 5 minutes.

If using, add the butter or coconut oil to a microwave-safe measuring cup with the remaining chocolate chips. Melt the remaining chocolate in the microwave in 20 second intervals, stirring after each round.

Drizzle the melted chocolate over the croissants and serve warm.

Chef's Tip:
Be sure not to add too many chocolate chips to the crescent dough*. If you add too much chocolate, it will make the dough difficult to roll and may cause the chocolate to leak out while they bake. It's essential that the chocolate stay inside of the dough rolls, or the croissants may burn in the oven. If you keep the chocolate to the recommended 1 tablespoon of chips per croissant, you should be good!

Croissant Day Card

National Broken Heart Day Card

National Broken Heart Day Fact Sheet

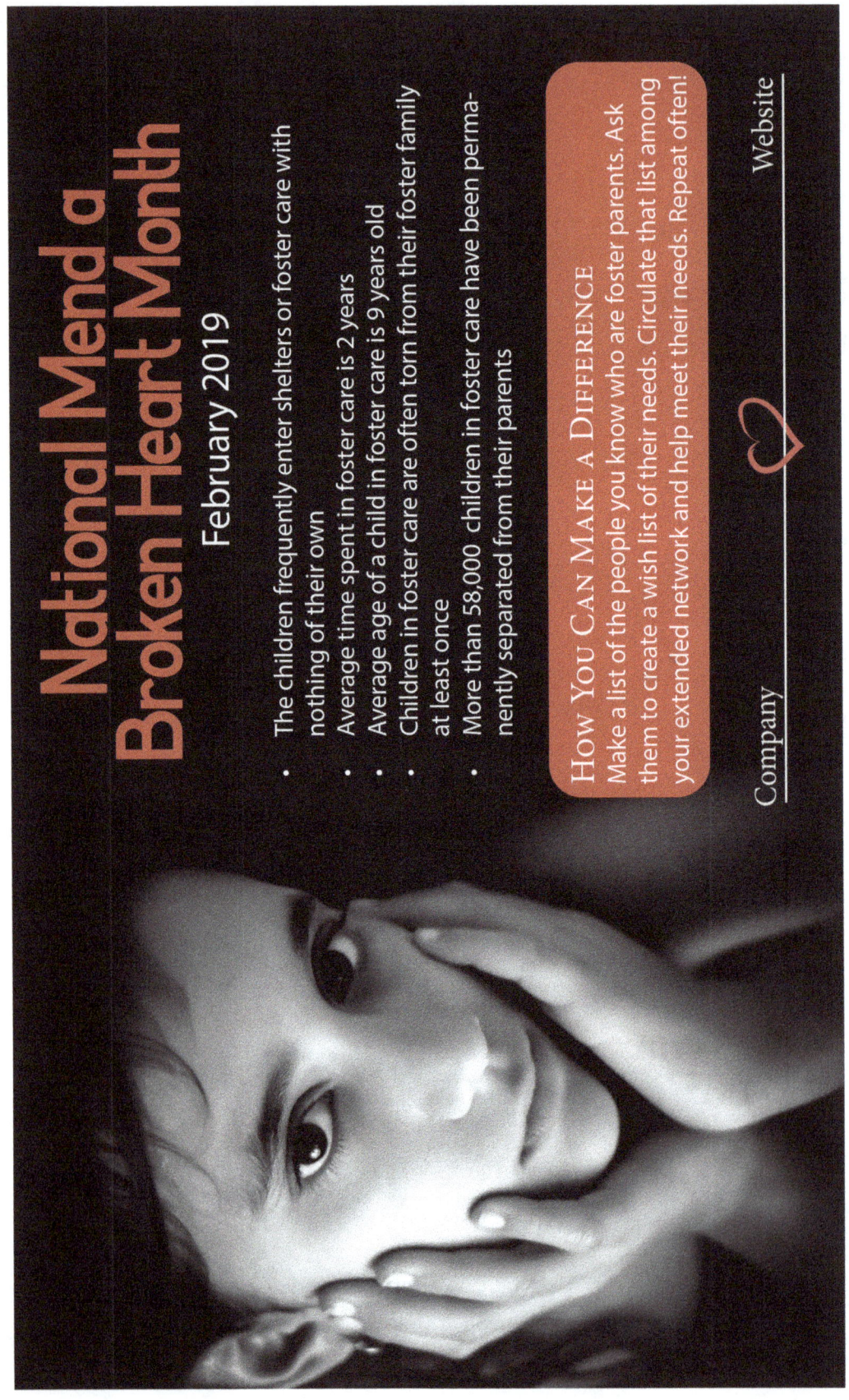

How To Organize a Drive

Whether you seek donations of large items such as mattresses or small items such as clothing, a drive is one of the easiest ways to accomplish your goals. Your steps to a successful drive may vary with the reason for your drive, but the basic planning … hardly ever vary.

1. Decide on the subject and recipient of your drive
   Find a worthwhile cause or organization that you wish to support. Check with your local chamber of commerce or city officials for a list of organizations requesting donations if you don't already have one in mind. Then contact them for more information on what their needs are and how to proceed.

2. Gather your support team

   Select your committee. Donation drives, while fun, do require a bit of organization and planning to be successful. With a proper support team in place and everyone assigned a specific task your drive will be well on the way to accomplishing all you hope to achieve.

   Some possible team members should include:
   - Chairperson to oversee all the details and answer questions
   - Charity drive liaison
   - Advertising/Marketing Coordinator
   - Photographer
   - Donation Coordinator
   - Chief of storing donations
   - Coordinator of packing and transportation to the non-profit organization

3. Set your goals

   Plan how you will affect your drive. Determine the amount you want to raise. Encourage your team to strive to surpass your goals.

   Determine if you will offer matching gift opportunities and identify companies who might be willing to participate. If you are seeking physical items, your matching donation might be $1 for every specific number of donated items. As an example, for every five pairs of shoes they will match with $1 dollar.

4. Get the word out

   Marketing will enable you to meet those pre-determined expectations. Begin by distributing flyers and letting the media know the importance of your drive.

   There are numerous ways to generate excitement and visibility throughout the drive. Here's just two:
   - Film or take photos of the piles of supplies being sorted, filled backpacks, volunteers, children or other media interest grabs.
   - Use social media to spread the word.

5. Accept donations

Will you have multiple drop-off locations or just one central hub? Possible locations could include churches, schools, restaurants, stores, and corporations. Be sure your donation boxes are uniformly identifiable. This will make it easy for your donators to know what they are looking for when trying to find your donation collection box.

Create an online donation platform for those who wish to contribute but wouldn't otherwise. Use relatable verbiage like "$30 will purchase one box of food to feed a family of four for a week" or "$5 will provide 1 notebook, a packet of pencils, and 2 erasers" will encourage generous giving.

6. Organize and deliver your donations

As donations are received, take time to run through the donations to look for items that cannot be used once delivered to the nonprofit. Consider taking photos of mounds of supplies to share with the media and support organizations before they are sorted into the way that the receiving nonprofit has requested. See the timeline in the following pages for ideas to consider as you plan your drive.

7. Deliver

Delivering your donations is a great way to engage others and generate additional attention for the success of your drive. Consider inviting donors to assist in the delivery of the donations for a hands-on feel or encourage your team to wear their company or school t-shirts while sorting and delivering your donations for additional recognition of their support.

8. Evaluate

Timeline:

6–8 Weeks

Identify potential community partners (companies, retail businesses, agencies, chambers of commerce, council on corporate volunteerism, faith-based groups, colleges, labor unions) and others to:

- Receive and deliver school supply collections
- Serve as collection or drop-off centers
- Provide transportation and logistical support
- Donate warehouse or parking lot space for an event
- Help promote the project, e.g., media, publicity volunteers
- Create a list with information on all partners, including: name, address, contact name(s), phone, e-mail address, category, website, notes
- Schedule face-to-face or phone meetings to discuss a project idea. Determine next steps for each member of the planning committee (their role, time commitment, how to manage collection of supplies)

4–6 Weeks

Brief other staff or committee members on all aspects of the project and involve them in any further planning and preparation. Schedule post-event meeting, to ensure that committee members are available to debrief and attend to follow-up tasks.

- Draft agenda for the day of an event

- Notify your marketing & communication departments for PR/media plan
- Discuss documentation (photos, video) of an event
- Recruit a volunteer photographer if possible
- If needed, verify need for photo a release form
- If needed, order event t-shirts, signage or other collateral, as needed
- Plan any transportation and other logistics needed

2–4 Weeks
- Visit collection sites. Address any remaining questions and concerns
- Recruit volunteers
- Secure attendance of all dignitaries as needed for an event's agenda
- Draft or secure talking points for dignitaries to include in the run of show document
- Finalize task lists and make sure all committee members are comfortable with scope of work

1–2 Weeks
- Confirm all final details
- Make sure you will have tables and chairs for all donation drop-off stations
- Confirm materials needed, will be onsite
- Pack a "project kit" to include things such as:
    - ✓ Signage and banners
    - ✓ Pens, markers
    - ✓ Tape
    - ✓ Extra paper/card stock/poster board
    - ✓ Flyers about the donation drive

Sample Financial Gift Form

(Organization's Logo)

Yes! I want to partner with (Organization)! Below is my tax-deductible gift.

Please fill out the form below and fax/mail to:

Organization: _____

Address: _____

City, State Zip: _____

Phone/Fax Number: _____

My Gift:

☐ $25   ☐ $100

☐ $50   ☐ Other $ _____

☐ $75

Contact Information:

Name _____

Address _____

City/State/Zip _____

Phone _____

Email _____

☐ Please check this box if you prefer to keep your gift anonymous.

Payment Options:

☐ Enclosed is my check or money order made payable to_____.

☐ I wish to donate by credit card. Below is my credit card information.

☐ Visa ☐ MasterCard ☐ American Express

Card number (16 digits) _____ Expiration (mm/yy) _____

Card holder name _____

Cardholder Signature _____

☐ My Employer has a Matching Gift Program. Enclosed with my donation is my company's form.

☐ This gift is designated (check one if applicable)

☐ In honor of: _____

☐ In memory of: _____

Please notify:

Name _____

Address _____

City/State/Zip _____

Foster Parent Facts

Courtesy of Adoption.org https://adoption.org/requirements-foster-parent

What Are the Requirements To Be a Foster Parent?

Perhaps you are thinking about becoming a foster parent, but you are not sure if you could do it or not. Maybe you don't think you are qualified or eligible for whatever reasons. Before you dismiss the idea, it's worth reading further to see just what the requirements to be a foster parent really are. You might be surprised to find out that you are eligible after all. The requirements are not all that restrictive per se, however, there are a lot of rules and policies to follow once you are licensed as a foster parent.

There are often misconceptions about who can become a foster parent. Some people assume that you have to be a 30 something year old, married, wealthy couple who own a large home and fancy car to care for foster children. Reality is that foster parents are made up of people from all different walks of life. There are many different people from different families, backgrounds, careers, gender, race, marital status, and life situations that choose to be foster parents. The laws vary somewhat from state to state, but here is a list of general guidelines to help you determine if you might meet the eligibility requirements or not. You will also want to verify with your local county or agency before you proceed as some agencies may have additional standards. You can also view state specific criteria here.

1. Age

    Most states have a minimum age requirement to be considered as a foster parent. In most states, an applicant must be at least 21 years old, however, in some states the minimum age requirement is only 18 years old. Of course, you should also consider your own level of maturity, personal situation, and readiness to foster before you apply. Even though your state may allow you to foster children at the age of 18, you may find it challenging trying to parent a foster child who is only a few years younger than yourself.

2. Criminal Background Check

    All states require you to pass a criminal background check before caring for foster children for obvious reasons. They want to ensure that children will be placed in safe and stable home environments, with someone who can meet their needs. Each state has different standards for what they consider passing. Minor infractions may not automatically disqualify someone from being licensed, especially if it occurred more than five or 10 years ago for example. However, there will be certain crimes, especially crimes against children or involving violence that will permanently prevent someone from ever becoming a foster parent. Bottom line: if your background check is clean there is nothing to worry about. If there is something minor on your record and it was a long time ago, you can check with your local state laws to see if it will prevent you from becoming a foster parent or not.

3. Income

    Many people think they could never be a foster parent because they don't make enough money. Truth is, there is no specific income requirement to be a foster parent. Most states just require that applicants provide proof of adequate monthly income to meet their family's needs. They basically want to ensure that you can pay your mortgage or rent, utilities, and provide basic needs such as food and clothes for the children. You may need to provide copies of tax returns, pay stubs, and utility bills as proof of adequate income.

4. Housing

   There is no requirement for you to live in a mansion or certain size home or even to own your own home at all. Foster parents can rent homes or apartments and that is perfectly acceptable. Whatever your place of residency may be, you will just want to make sure that it meets the safety standards and that there is room for the number of children you wish to be licensed for. Each state will have specific rules regarding how many kids can share a room and if children of different genders and ages can share rooms. You will need to prove that you have adequate space for each child that meets these guidelines. Your housing will also need to meet the safety standards such as adequate supply of safe drinking water, electricity, smoke detectors, etc. Your home does not need to be new or immaculate. In most cases, pets are acceptable as well. People may worry they won't be approved because of their animals, but if they are friendly and up to date on their vaccinations, pets should not be a hindrance either.

5. Health

   Some people don't think they could be a foster parent because they are diabetic, have high blood pressure, or some other medical diagnosis. There are no specific diseases that will automatically prevent someone from being a foster parent. Most states just require applicants to be healthy enough to meet the needs of the children. If your medical conditions are managed well with treatment and you are stable enough to care for children daily than your health should not be an issue. You may be asked to provide a letter or statement from your physician indicating that you are in good health or that you are fit to care for children. Particularly they are concerned about mental health diagnoses and making sure those conditions are managed and stable before being licensed as a foster parent.

6. Transportation

   Owning a car and having a valid driver's license is beneficial, but not always required to be a foster parent. Obviously if you are planning to drive, your license must be valid and you must have automobile insurance. Check with your specific state and agency regarding what they require for transportation. In some areas, you may only need to provide proof of reliable transportation which could be access to the bus, subway, train, taxi, relative, neighbor, etc. Having your own vehicle is preferred though since there are many places to transport the children such as doctors' appointments, therapy appointments, visits, school, etc.

7. Marital Status

   I've heard people say, "I'm single, I can't be a foster parent," but in fact a person can be single and still be a foster parent. There are many single foster parents and the ones I know personally do an excellent job caring for their children. You do not need to be married or to be a couple to be a foster parent. A few states may require couples applying together to be married but not in all states.

8. Citizenship/Residency

   You do not necessarily have to be a US citizen to be a foster parent. This is one question I had and was pleasantly surprised about the answer since I was Canadian and concerned I would not be approved. Even though you may not have to be a citizen, applicants will need to at least be a legal resident, and in some cases, may need to have been a resident of that state for a specific number of years before applying. A few states also have requirements of being able to read, write, and speak English. Basically, it is important for foster parents to be able to communicate with the children they will be caring for.

9. Experience/Training

   You do not need to have previous parenting experience, although I'm sure it would help. Regardless of how much parenting experience you have, everyone must take the required foster parent training classes. These classes and the number of hours required will vary from state to state. These classes should be offered by your local county or foster care agency.

10. Home Study

    Before anyone can be licensed as a foster parent, they must have an approved home study. Your home study will be completed by the county or agency that you will be fostering through. The assessor will come to your home for one or more visits to talk with you and your family. During that time, they will also look at your home to ensure that all the safety standards are met and that there is a place for the children to sleep etc. They will most likely ask many personal questions about your family, so they can get to know you better and determine what kind of foster parents you would be. If you are open and honest with them, you should not have any problems. Chances are if you meet all the previously listed requirements to become a foster parent, you should have little to no difficulty passing the home study.

    Hopefully now you have a better understanding of what the requirements are to become licensed as a foster parent and whether you qualify or not. Because laws and information are constantly changing and vary from state to state, always make sure you verify everything with your state and county or agency.

Sherri Eppley is a wife and mother to two amazing children. As a foster and adoptive parent, she strives to raise awareness of all issues related to foster care and adoption. Her passions include her family, church, MOPS, and helping people in any ways she can.

Freedom Day Social Media Image

While these two graphics, at a glance, may not look different, they are, in fact, sized appropriately for each social media website. If you would like any of the full-size images provided in this book or to have them customized for you please email Ginger at designer@documeantdesigns.com.

Facebook Graphic

Twitter Graphic

Random Acts of Kindness Cards

Print several on business card cardstock sheet, separate them, and hand them out on the bus, at the grocery store, at the toll booth, at a plant or children's nursery (the employees and teachers will love it), or any number of other places you go during Random Acts of Kindness Day and Week. When you do something nice, just before handing them the card, it will give you both a sense of goodwill. Even a random hug, could make someone's day.

Customize any of the designs in this book with your business name and URL. Need help? Contact Ginger for assistance.

Polar Bear Fun Fact Sheet

Polar Bear Flyer

Polar Bear Day reminds us that our words aren't enough to protect these species—every individual no matter how far he lives ought to do something on its own that adds real value to his efforts. To put it in the words of Amstup, a leading polar bear researcher, *"If you think there is nothing you can do, then you will do nothing,"* he said. *"So start doing something. Make a personal commitment and share what you are doing with your colleagues, your church, your synagogue and your other social networks."*

Your Action or Inaction Will Make the Difference!

The prime responsibility lies on the humans for several arctic mammals let alone polar bears have suffered badly in the last couple of centuries. Something needs to be done on priority basis before it's too late and it doesn't matter if your habitat is miles away from polar bear's habitat.

- Begin using zero carbon technology in vehicles
- Plant more and more trees
- Stop hunting
- Speak up for wildlife

COMPANY NAME

wishes you a

Happy Polar Bear Day!

February 27th

Fun Facts About Name Day Graphics

Facebook Graphic

Twitter Graphic

90+ Twitter Tools

Courtesy of Buffer https://blog.bufferapp.com/free-twitter-tools

You'll find all the links to these tools in Appendix D.

Analytics

1. Daily 140: Recent follows and favorites of 3 tweeps of your choosing
   Find three folks on Twitter, and Daily 140 emails you once-a-day with all the new people they've followed and tweets they've favorited.

2. My Top Tweet: Your Top 10 list of tweets
   Find anyone's Top 10 tweets, ordered by engagement.

3. SocialBro: Analytics, optimization, and more
   A nearly all-in-one platform for all things Twitter. The free plan comes with analytics, best time to tweet, follow/unfollow tools, and community segmentation.

4. Riffle: Data visualizations for any Twitter user
   This browser plugin reveals vast insights into any Twitter user you choose. Discover statistics, popular hashtags, most shared links, connected profiles, and much more.

5. Twitonomy: Detailed analytics on users and tweets
   A dashboard of analytics for whichever Twitter user you choose (even yours). Analyzes profiles, tweets, engagement, and more.

6. Klout: Twitter scores
   Track your influencer score (on a scale of 1-100) and use the Klout dashboard to create and schedule new tweets.

7. SumAll: Email reports for Twitter stats
   Sync your Twitter to SumAll, and start seeing daily or weekly emails on how your followers are growing, your mentions, and your engagement.

8. SocialRank: Follower analysis to find your most awesome fans
   Receive a sorted list of your best followers, most influential followers, and most engaged followers. Useful to track the important people to engage with on Twitter.

9. Klear: Social media analytics & a Twitter resume
   Plug in your Twitter account to see a snapshot of who you follow, which demographics you fit, who's in your close network, and more.

10. Bluenod: Community visualization
    Type in a user or hashtag and see a detailed map or visualization about the community around the user or the people using the hashtag.

11. Twitter account home: The official overview of your Twitter profile
    Head to analytics.twitter.com for a detailed overview of all your activity in the past 28 days, including your top tweets, top mentions, and top followers.

12. Social Bearing: Powerful search for tweets and profiles
    Search Twitter keywords, locations, usernames, interests, or followers, then use your new-found knowledge to analyze your fellow tweeps or find new ones to follow.

13. Stats for Twitter: Beautiful iOS app to analyze yours and others's Twitter accounts
    See a visual breakdown of all sorts of Twitter stats: Followers analyzed by activity and popularity, competitors shown side-by-side with your account, etc.

Chat

14. Beatstrap: Team liveblogging
    Cover live news, sports, and events through Twitter, via hashtags, and collaborate with your team on the coverage. Completed "Beats" come with an embed code.

15. TweetChat: Twitter chat management
    Log in to follow a specific hashtag, hang out in a room that collects the hashtagged tweets for you, and reply as you like (with the hashtag added automatically to your tweet).

16. Chat Salad: A calendar of Twitter chats
    See upcoming Twitter chats and when they're scheduled, as well as the hashtags they use (so you can follow along).

17. Twubs: Twitter chat homepages
    Register a hashtag for your chat and collect/view the tweets from one location.

18. Nurph: Chat planning and organizing
    Nurph channels let you plan and organize your chat, complete with follow-up stats and replays.

19. TwChat: Real-time chat rooms for Twitter chats
    Submit your hashtag. Enter your chat room. Have fun!

Discovery

20. Nuzzel: Discover what your friends are reading
    As described by Twitter's Joanna Geary, "find out what's trending among the people the people you follow follow." Make sense? Translation: Content discovery from friends and friend of friends.

21. BuzzSumo: Find influencers, topic-by-topic
    Type in a keyword to see which voices get the most shares on Twitter. Find influencers, sniff out headline ideas, and learn what works on Twitter and who's working it.

22. Swayy: What your followers are interested in
    See the content that your followers recommend plus the topics they most enjoy. View it all via the dashboard or from a daily email digest.

23. Twipho: Searchable Twitter feed of photos
    Search by keyword or by location to find photos shared on Twitter.

24. Digg Deeper: The best stories from your friends
    An algorithmic display of the top articles and links that your Twitter followees have shared. Pair with News.me: a daily email newsletter of what your friends share on Twitter.

25. The Latest: A museum for the day's best Twitter links
    A real-time, constantly updated list of the most interesting links on Twitter, culled from the accounts of interesting people

26. Twurly: Daily email of top Twitter links
    An easy way to stay on top of the best links in your timeline. Twurly analyzes the popularity and page authority of the links so you only see the best.

27. Filta: Bio search all your followers
    Curious which of your followers are into football? Use Filta to search the bios of all your followers for any keyword you want.

28. Hash: Top stories on Twitter

A visual look at the leading stories and hashtags on Twitter. Available on the web and as an iOS app.

29. Brook: Customized Twitter digests of top tweets from top tweeps
    Receive a daily email of the five best tweets from the Twitter users you choose.

Follow/Unfollow

30. Crowdfire: Powerful follower management
    Prune your list of those you follow by seeing who follows you back, who's recently unfollowed you, and who's inactive, plus build a whitelist of accounts you'd always like to follow no matter what.

31. ManageFlitter: Follow/unfollow in bulk
    Segment your followers according to a number of factors: last tweet, follower count, location, language and whether or not they follow you back.

32. Tweepi: Tidy up who you follow
    Cleanup inactive follows, flush those who don't follow back, and reciprocate someone else's follow — all done in bulk and with a few clicks of a checkbox.

33. Unfollowers: In-depth follow/unfollow
    Get a complete breakdown of those you follow, and unfollow, with ease.

34. DoesFollow: See who follows whom
    Does A follow B? Does Bill Gates follow Skrillex? Does Guy Kawasaki follow Jay Baer?

35. Commun.it: Complete follower management dashboard
    See all the information on all your followers – top tweets, influence, and more.

36. T.U.N.S.: Twitter Unfollow Notification Service
    Receive an email every time someone unfollows you.

37. Twindr: Tindr for unfollowing people (iOS)
    Swipe left to unfollow, swipe right to keep following.

38. Toolset.co: Twitter toolset for finding people to follow or unfollow
    Simple tools to grow your followers. Copy the follow list of another user, find users to follow based on keyword or device.

39. Linkreaser: Grow your following by finding accounts based on keyword
    Share a keyword, and Linkreaser will find tweets and influencers you might like to see and follow.

40. FollowFly: What else are Twitter users sharing?
    Search Twitter users, find their best content on Twitter and beyond – Facebook, Instagram, YouTube, SoundCloud, and Reddit AMAs are currently supported.

Hashtags

41. Rite tag: Hashtag recommender
    Plug in a hashtag and see feedback on the tag's reach and popularity as well as suggestions for some alternatives to try. Complete with pretty colors to see at-a-glance which hashtags are best.

42. Hashtagify.me: Complete analytics into any hashtag
    Enter a hashtag to discover related tags, recent conversations, usage patterns, and influencers.

43. Seen: Hashtag-based curation

Collect the media that was shared with a certain hashtag, then rank the results. Share your curation with friends and followers.

44. Tagboard: Mood boards for hashtags
    Enter in a hashtag and Tagboard will pull all the most recent and relevant content into a highly useful board of tweets and visuals.

Images

45. Pablo: Create beautiful social media images in 30 seconds
    A tool we build here at Buffer, Pablo lets you quickly share a quote or build an image with beautiful backgrounds from UnSplash and the best, catchiest fonts. Customize with your logo, too.

46. Spruce: Text over image
    Create an attention-getting image with Spruce's simple and quick image-making app.

47. Twitshot: See & share the images from any web page
    Give Twitshot a URL, and it will pull in all the images associated with that page, giving you an easy option to see what to share.

48. Share As Image: Highlight text, create image
    Highlight text from whatever page you're on and click the Share As Image bookmarklet to toss that text directly into an eye-catching image.

49. Finch: Discover and curate images on Twitter
    Finch turns Twitter into streams of endless photos of anything.

Mentioning & Monitoring

50. Warble: Alerts every time your blog posts are shared
    Get an email whenever someone shares from your website—even if they don't mention your username or if they use a link shortener. Warble also does full keyword, mention, and hashtag tracking.

51. Keyhole: LIke Google Alerts for Twitter
    Ask Keyhole to notify you whenever a particular keyword, hashtag, or URL is mentioned. Helpful to track mentions of your own name or your company's blog or campaign.

52. The One Million Tweetmap: Geolocated, real-time tweet monitoring
    Track and follow keywords as they're tweeted in real-time and at real places. Zoom in to a geotargeted area for super fine results.

53. Twilert: Real-time email alerts for keywords
    Track keywords on Twitter and receive an email notification every time they're mentioned. Great for keeping an eye on company names, new products, and branded hashtags.

54. Mention: Monitor your mentions
    A listening tool for keeping up with all your mentions on Twitter. Tracks, analyzes, and displays any number of keywords via the Mention dashboard or via email digests.

55. MentionMapp: The web of you and those you mention
    Get a visualization map of you and all the people you mention (and they people they mention).

56. Twazzup: Real-time keyword monitoring
    Search and track any keyword, username, or hashtag. See a results page full of relevant tweets, user accounts, and influencers.

Scheduling

57. Buffer: Schedule your tweets (plus a whole lot more)
   Simple social media management. Fill a queue of tweets, analyze their performance, and find new, hand-picked stories to share.

   We also take a lot of inspiration from the great work of Hootsuite and Sprout Social, which offer an amazing list of management tools.

58. Tweet4me: Scheduled tweets via DM
   Send a direct message to the Tweet4me account, use shorthand and prefixes to denote when to share, and let Tweet4me schedule and send the tweet for you.

Timing

59. Followerwonk: Search Twitter bios and analyze your followers
   Every analysis imaginable for your Twitter feed, your profile, your followers, and your competitors.

60. Tweriod: Find the best times to tweet
   Tweriod analyzes the tweets you send and your followers' tweets to find the optimal time for engagement.

Trending

61. Trends24: Detailed breakdowns of trending terms
   See trending terms from the last — you guessed it — 24 hours, broken out hour-by-hour and country-by-country. Enlightening for social media campaigns and geographic/timing research.

62. Trendsmap: Monitoring for local Twitter trends
   A zoomable map that shows popular hashtags and terms from anywhere in the world with easy-click buttons to hone in on My City, My Region, and more.

63. iTrended: Did it trend?
   Search the past 15 days to find whether certain keywords trended or not.

Top Clients

64. Tweetdeck: The king of Twitter clients
   Via the app or the web, stay on top of your Twitter stream with Tweetdeck's organization and tracking tools. Split your stream into segmented columns to stay engaged with what's important.

65. YoruFukurou – Twitter client
   A native Twitter client for Mac OS X. Dashboard views of incoming tweets, lists, and searches, split across multiple tabs. Comes highly recommended from Kottke.org.

66. Happy Friends: Mailbox-type reader
   Pick the friends you want to hear from. Never miss their tweets. View all their activity via an inbox-style layout with nested updates.

67. Twitterific: Twitter client for iOS
   Powerful Twitter client for iPhone, iPad, and Apple Watch, with cool features like color-coded timelines and muffled keywords or hashtags.

68. Twitter Dashboard: Connecting businesses with their fans, customers, and community.

Twitter's own client for businesses to manage their accounts, schedule tweets, view analytics and much more.

69. Hash: Today's talking points
    Hash is a Twitter client that focuses on key topics people are talking about in real-time

Miscellaneous Tools

70. Like Explorer: See shares per article
    Type in a URL. See the share numbers. Simple.
71. Twitter Feed – Serve your feed automatically to Twitter (and others)
    Post a new article on your site. Send a tweet automatically.
72. TW Birthday: Dig up the date someone joined Twitter (even if they won't say)
    For those who omit the "date joined" on their profile, there's still a way to discover it. See how long your new favorite follow has been tweeting or when a new profile officially landed.
73. Bio is Changed: be alerted when someone changes their Twitter bio (good for job moves)
    Rather self-descriptive, this tool updates you when someone changes their Twitter bio. Useful if you'd like to track job moves and major news or even to learn from how people craft unique Twitter bios.
74. IFTTT and . . .
75. Zapier: Automate your tweeting
    Connect multiple apps in unique ways to your Twitter account. For example, post your Instagram pictures as native Twitter photos.
76. Be Present: Track how fast you respond on Twitter
    Real-time reports on your response time, response rate, and performance based on industry benchmarks. Also, really pretty to look at.
77. SavePublishing: Tweetable snippets on any website
    Install the bookmarklet, and you can reveal any tweetable sentences (140 characters or fewer) from any article.
78. GroupTweet: Collaborate with teammates on one account
    Let your teammates and coworkers share to the same account automatically with zero password-sharing. GroupTweet can even append usernames on to the end of individual tweets.
79. Storify: Beautiful Twitter storytelling
    Grab any number of tweets and media elements and place them all into a Storify collection that you can embed and share anywhere.
80. Tweet Topic Explorer: A word cloud per user
    Discover the most-used words of any user you choose (even you).
81. Listen to Twitter: Listen to the sentiment of tweets
    Type in a keyword and hear an audio track based on the sentiment of the tweets with that keyword.
82. Thunderclap: Automated advocacy
    Start a new campaign on Thunderclap, and if you get enough supporters to signup, Thunderclap will send your message out automatically through all your supporters' Twitter accounts.
83. Periscope & Meerkat: Livestreaming
    Live stream video of whatever you're up to.

84. Twitterfav: Automatic favorites and RTs
    Preselect tweets to be favorites or RT'ed based on rules you create.
85. Click to Tweet: Get people tweeting your content
    Add a highlighted snippet of easily-tweetable text to your website or blog post.
86. Bedazzle: Rich text editor for Twitter, using unicode
    Tons of options to make what looks like fancy fonts and styles in your tweet text (it's really just unicode characters). Looks great on Macs, and perhaps not so much on Windows PCs.
87. Pullquote: Grab quotes of text from any web page and share easily
    Available as Chrome extension, iOS app, and bookmarklet.
88. Who Tweeted It First: Find a story's origin
    Enter a keyword to see which person was the first to tweet it.
89. Little Pork Chop: Tweet storm
    Write more than 140 characters, and Little Pork Chop chops your text into Twitter-sized snippets, posting them all one after the other.
90. Hubbble: Favorite reminder system
    Favorite as many things as you'd like, and Hubbble will email you later to remind you to follow-up on your faves.
91. Nudge: Reminders to engage on Twitter
    Select tweets that you can boomerang back for followup later on.
92. SocialHunt: Track all activity for up to 5 tweeps
    Receive an email every time someone shares to Twitter. Set the frequency from "now" to "daily."
93. Twitter Bookmarks: Save your favorite tweets
    Twitter Bookmarks is an easy way to create bookmarks to your favorite things on Twitter.

Twitter Tips

1. You don't have to read every tweet
2. Collect your must-read Twitter accounts in a list
3. New to Twitter? Respond to everyone and everything
4. Consistency is king! Make your job easier by using scheduling software
5. Create a strong and complete bio
6. Engage others directly
7. Understand and use @ replies
8. It's OK to tweet the same thing multiple times
9. Set aside your follower-following ratio and just follow
10. Find out what lists you're on
11. Use hashtags
12. The best tweet times are on weekdays between 9am and 3pm EST. Forget Friday!
13. Use search operators
14. Use Advanced Search
15. Remove apps that have access to your account that are no long used by clicking "revoke access"
16. Turn off email notifications in your profile
17. Twitter texting is a good thing
18. Put limits on your social media usage, including Twitter
19. Go to settings to retrieve your tweet history
20. Subscribe to public lists
21. If you haven't tried out #Discover, you need to do it now
22. Use Twitter keyboard shortcuts
23. Create your own Twitter homepage
24. Find your most valuable followers
25. Disengage from the list of who you follow if they are not active

Holy Humor Month Jokes

1. Q. What did the Buddhist ask the hot dog vendor? A. Make me one with everything.
2. Q. What do you get when you cross a dyslexic, an insomniac, and an agnostic? A. Someone who lays awake at night wondering if there is a dog.
3. Q. What did the green grape say to the purple grape? A. OMG!!!!!!! BREATHE!! BREATHEEEEE!!!!!
4. Q. What's a pirate's favorite letter? A. You think it's R but it be the C.
5. I asked my daughter if she'd seen my newspaper. She told me that newspapers are old school. She said that people use tablets nowadays and handed me her iPad. The fly didn't stand a chance.
6. Q. Why is it a bad idea to insult an octopus? A. Because it is well armed.
7. The young mother asked her son, "Johnny, why did you put your teddy in the freezer?" He quickly replied, "I wanted a polar bear."
8. Q: Did you hear about the cheese factory that exploded in France? A. There was nothing left but de Brie.
9. Q: What's the best time to go to the dentist? A: Tooth hurty.
10. Q. Which rock group has four guys who can't sing or play instruments? A. Mount Rushmore.

National Beer Day Graphic

World Penguin Day Fun Facts

National Baby Sitters Day Emergency Contacts

EMERGENCY CONTACT LIST FOR CAREGIVERS

Mother
Work: Cell: Address:
Email:

Father
Work: Cell: Address:
Email:

Child: Child: Child:
Allergies: Allergies: Allergies:
Meds: Meds: Meds:

Medical Information
Pediatrician:
Dentist:
Specialist:
Preferred hospital:

Emergency Contact
Name: Address:
Work: Cell:
Email:
Relationship:

Emergency Phone Numbers
General: 911
Fire:
Police:
Poison Control: 1-800-222-1222

Where to find
Medical Authorization Form:

Insurance Information:

Car Insurance Coverage:

Emergency Plans:

company | website

Supply Chain Professionals Day Graphic

National Eat at a Food Truck Day Card

Food Truck Tweets

1. #eatatafoodtruck eat everything
2. Don't cook today! Support #foodtruck dining. Share the love.
3. I'm not counting calories today, I'm supporting #foodtruck day.
4. I'm dining out at my favorite #foodtruck. Will you join me?
5. #foodtruck dining is not for the finicky eater.
6. Coffee is food too on national #foodtruck dining day.
7. Eat at a #foodtruck! #yum
8. Let's stuff our faces on National #foodtruck day.
9. Food Truck Day Hashtags:
10. #neftd #food #foodie #foodtruck #foodtrucks #foodtruckfestival #yum #eatatafoodtruck

Medical Information Card

Print these cards double-sided on business card stock. The inside is on the next page.

Outside

MEDICATIONS: DOSAGE/FREQUENCY:

MEDICAL IDENTIFICATION CARD

company | website

Inside:

NAME: _____ DATE: _____

Emergency Contact: _____

Phone: _____

Physician: _____

Physician's Phone: _____

Contact Lenses: Y ☐   N ☐

Blood Type: _____

Medical Conditions: _____
_____
_____
_____
_____

Allergies: _____
_____
_____
_____

Tell an Old Joke Day Graphic

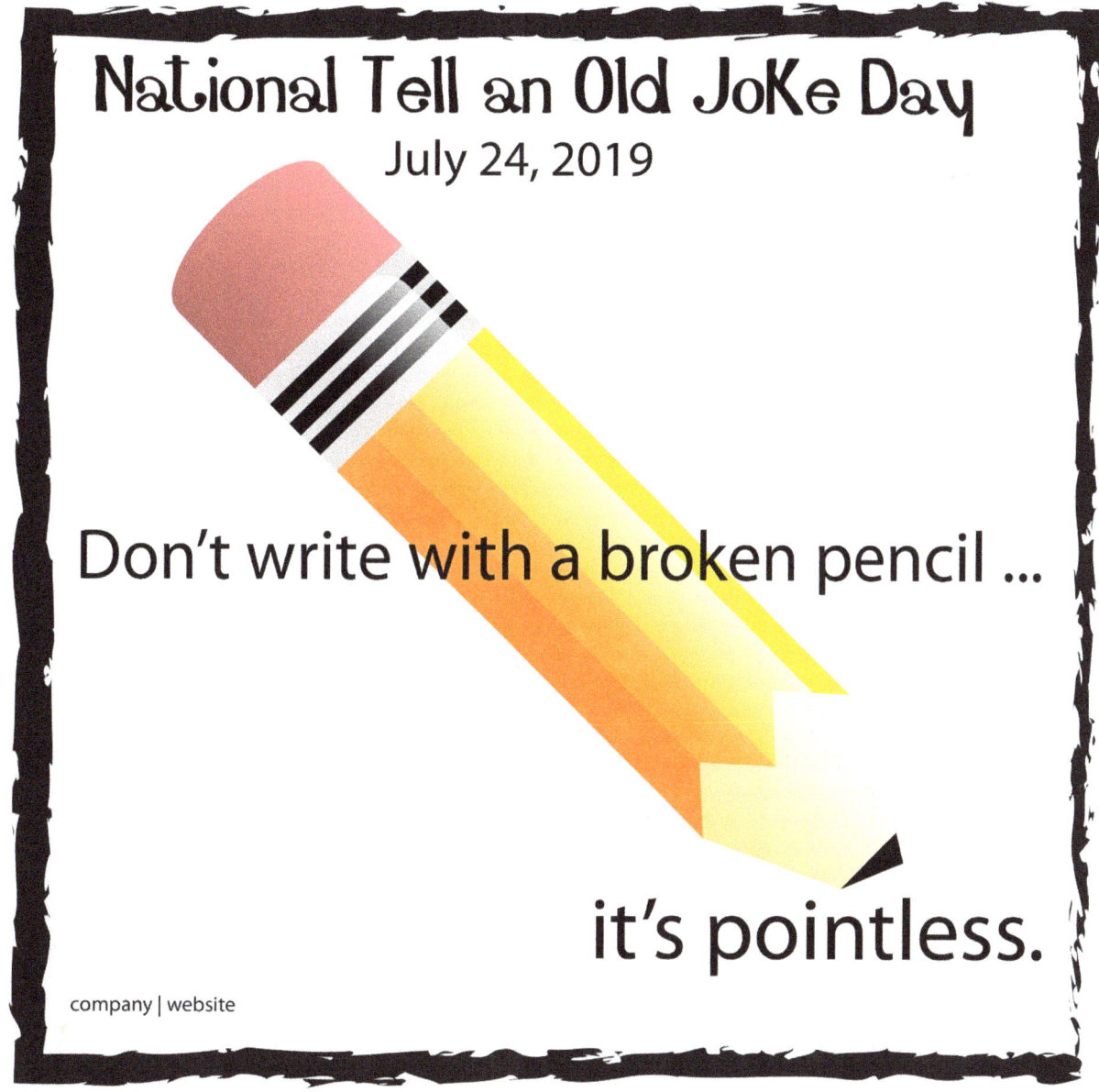

Customize any of the designs in this book with your business name and URL. Need help? Contact Ginger for assistance.

Pirate Event Poster

Avast ye maties!

Join us for a day's adventure in seeking treasure that will motivate you to grow your business.

Date:

Time:

Place:

Cost:

hosted by:
company • website

International Wave at Surveillance Day Graphic

Earth Hour Day Event Flyer

Positive Attitude Month Quotes

1. Who shoots at the mid-day sun, though he be sure he shall never hit the mark; yet as sure he is he shall shoot higher than who aims but at a bush. *Philip Sidney*
2. I'd rather be right than President. *Henry Clay*
3. Ah but a man's reach should exceed his grasp, Or what's a heaven for? *Robert Browning*
4. All ambitions are lawful except those which climb upwards on the miseries or credulities of mankind. *Joseph Conrad*
5. The artist is not a special kind of man, but every man is a special kind of artist. *Ananda Coomaraswamy*
6. I believe the right question to ask, respecting all ornament, is simply this: Was it done with enjoyment — was the carver happy while he was about it? *John Ruskin*
7. Positive thinking — the practice or result of concentrating one's mind on the good and constructive aspects of a matter so as to eliminate destructive attitudes and emotions. *Norman Vincent Peale,* The Power of Positive Thinking, *1952*
8. Mind over matter.
9. In front the sun climbs slow, how slowly,
   But westward, look the land is bright.
   Arthur Hugh Clough
10. Grab your coat, and get your hat,
    Leave your worry on the doorstep,
    Just direct your feet
    To the sunny side of the street.
    Dorothy Fields, On the Sunny Side of the Street, *1930*
11. Every time it rains, it rains
    Pennies from heaven.
    Don't you know each cloud contains
    Pennies from heaven?
    Johnny Burke, Pennies from Heaven, *1936*
12. You've got to ac-cent-tchu-ate the positive,
    Elim-my-nate the negative,
    Latch on to the affirmative,
    Don't mess with Mister In-between.
    Johnny Mercer, Ac-cent-tchu-ate the Positive, *1944*
13. Probable impossibilities are to be preferred to improbable possibilities. *Aristotle*
14. If a man will be content to begin with doubts, he shall end in certainties. *Francis Baacon*
15. For myself I am an optimist — it does not seem to be much use being anything else. *Winston Churchill*
16. Keep your face to the sunshine and you cannot see the shadow. Hellen Keller
17. If you think you are beaten, you are; If you think you dare not, you don't. If you'd like to win, but think you can't, It's almost a cinch you won't. If you think you'll lose, your lost, For out in the world we find Success beings with a fellow's will; It's all in the state of mind. *Walter D. Wintle*
18. You see things; and you say "Why?" But I dream things that never were; and I say "Why not?" *George Bernard Shaw*
19. Nothing happens unless first a dream. *Carl Sandburg*

20. There is no limit to what can be accomplished if it doesn't matter who gets the credit. *Ralph Waldo Emerson*
21. He who is waiting for something to turn up might start with his own shirt sleeves.
22. There is nothing like a dream to create the future. *Victor Hugo*
23. Far away there in the sunshine are my highest aspirations. I may not reach them but I can look up and see their beauty, believe in them and try to follow where they lead. *Louisa May Alcott*
24. Definiteness of purpose is the starting point of all achievement. *Clement Stone*
25. When your adversaries tell you that you can't go any further, just tell them to look behind you and see how far you've come.
26. Whatsoever thy hand findeth to do, do it with all thy might. *King Solomon*
27. Then the Lord said to Moses, "Quit praying and get the people moving! Forward march! (Exodus 14:15).
28. Every great man has been a self-starter.
29. Even if you're on the right track, you'll get run over if you just sit there.
30. Two bricklayers were asked what they were doing. The first replied, "I'm laying bricks"; the second responded, "I'm building a great cathedral." Same task, different perspective.
31. Here is the ladder to your dreams. The first rung is determination! And the second rung is dedication! The third is discipline! And the fourth rung is attitude! *Jesse Owen's coach before the Berlin Olympic Games*
32. [You] can alter [your] life by altering [your] attitude. *William James*
33. There is very little difference in people, but that little difference makes a big difference. The little difference is attitude. The big difference is whether it is positive or negative. *Clement Stone*
34. Assume a cheerfulness you do not feel and shortly you will feel the cheerfulness you assumed. *Chinese proverb*
35. Attitudes determine our altitudes.
36. I never did a day's work in my life — it was all fun. *Thomas Edison*
37. It's not the outlook, but the uplook that counts.

Appendix A: SAMPLES | 119

National Taco Day Coloring Page

Image by 1507kot at VectorStock.com

company website

Hockey Mask Day Template

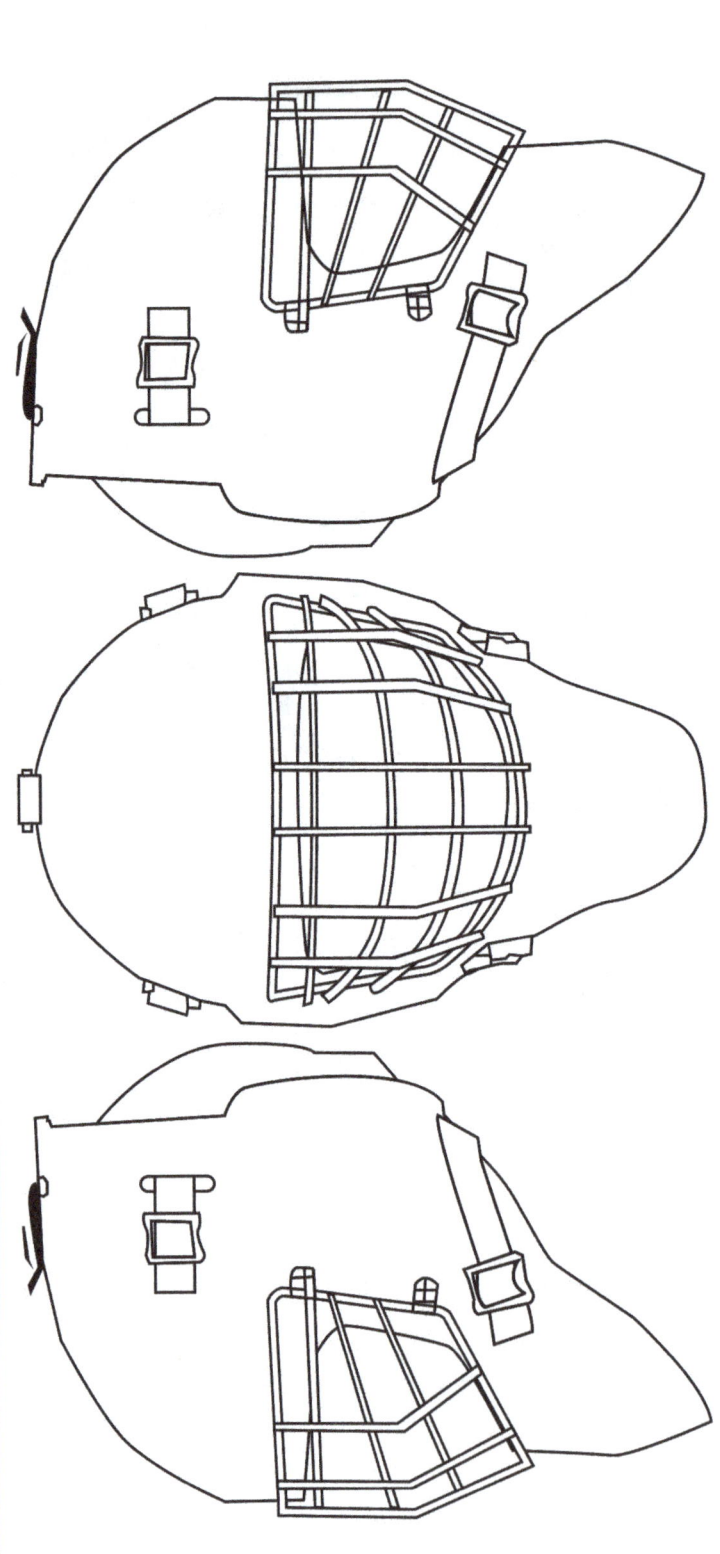

For Males

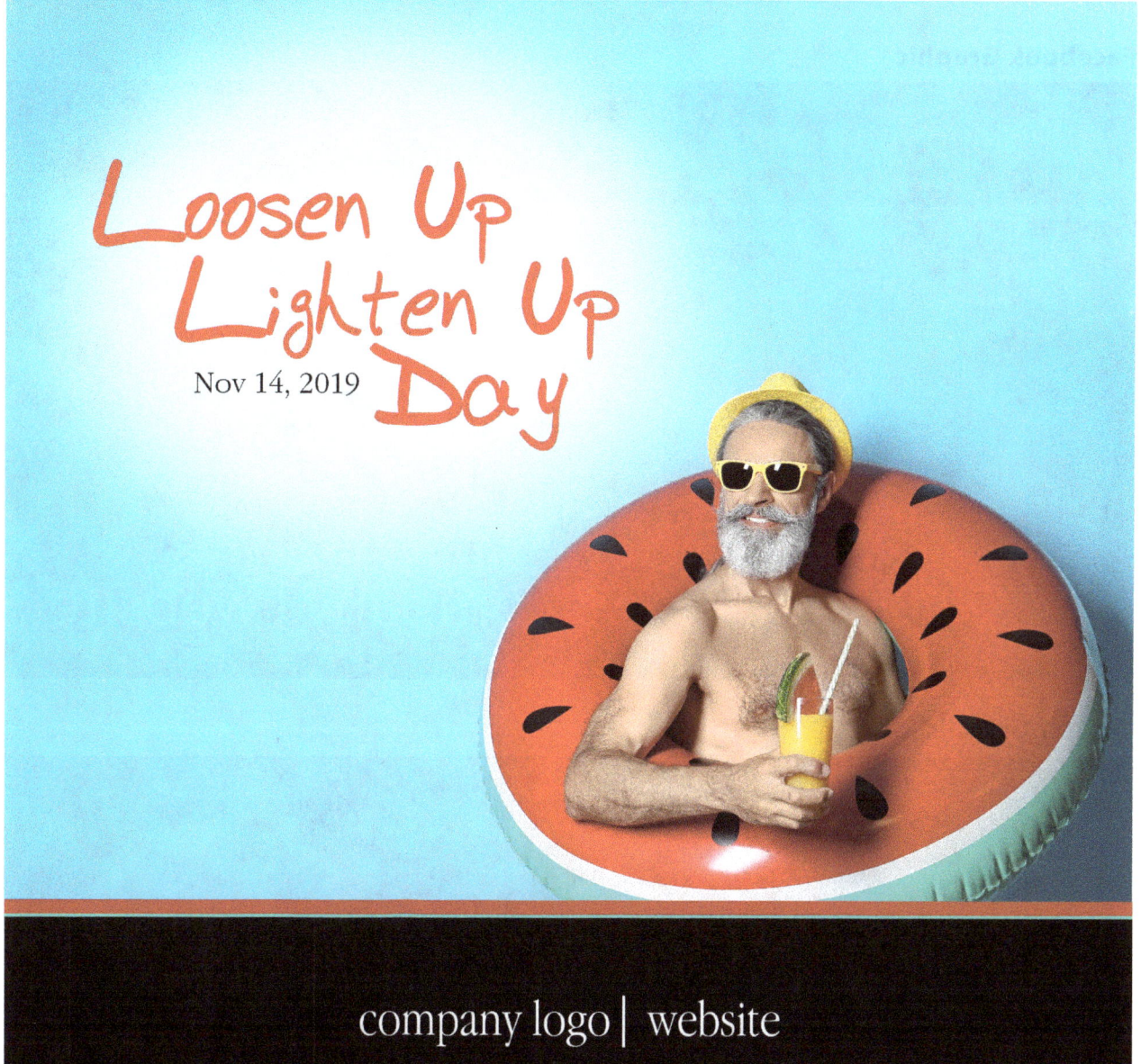

Name Your PC Day Graphic

Facebook Graphic

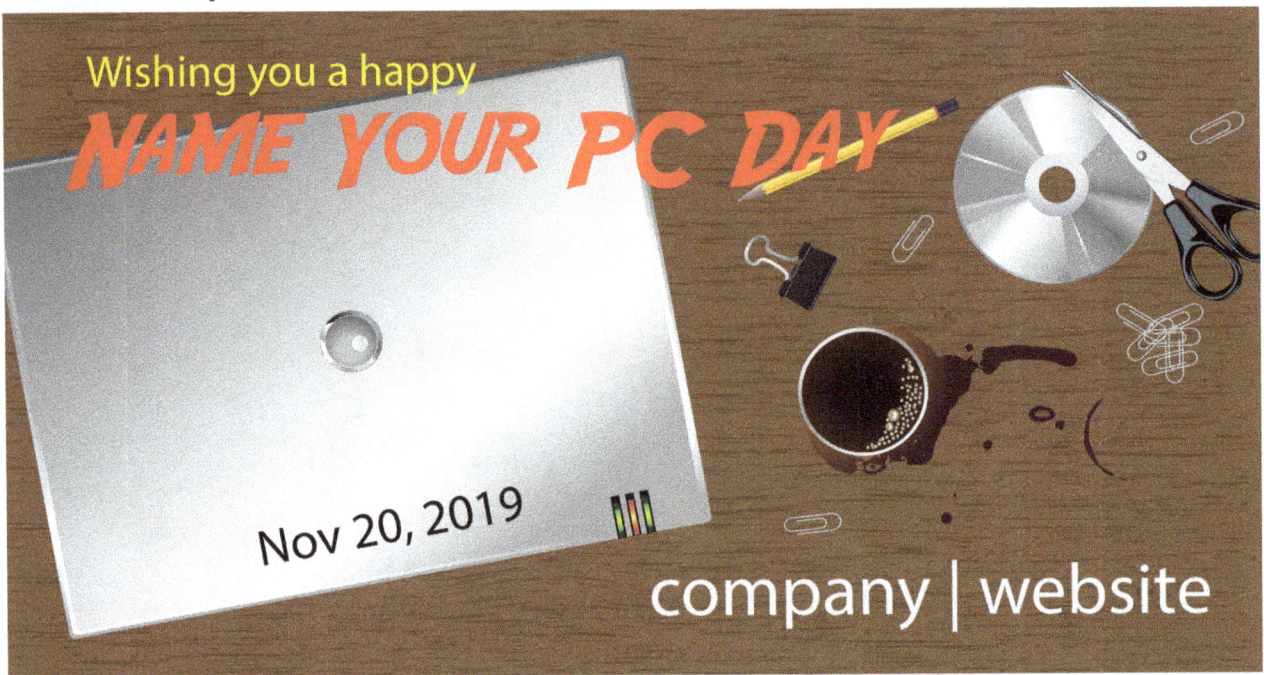

Twitter Graphic

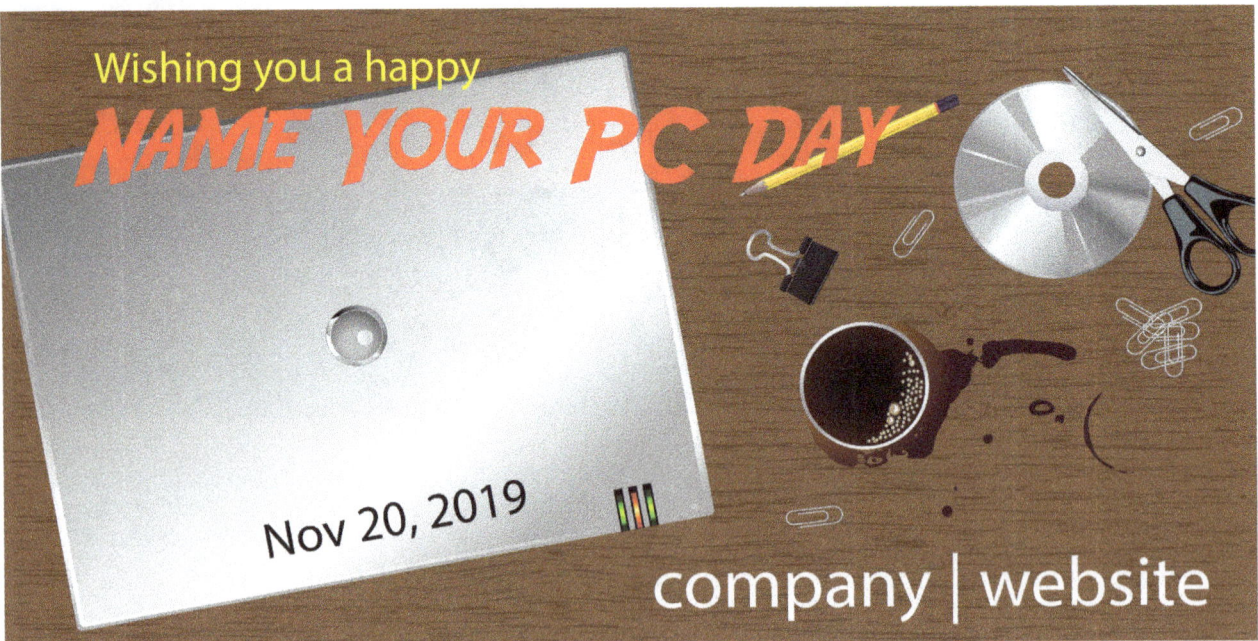

Freedom from Slavery Event Poster

National Fire Safety Counsel Day Graphic

Customize any of the designs in this book with your business name and URL. Need help? Contact Ginger for assistance.

Festivus Day Quotes

Customer Service

The most difficult thing in any negotiation, almost, is making sure that you strip it of the emotion and deal with the facts. *Howard Baker*

An apology is the superglue of life. It can repair just about anything. *Lynn Johnston*

Assumptions are the termites of relationships. *Henry Winkler*

There is only one boss. The customer. And he can fire everybody in the company from the chairman on down, simply by spending his money somewhere else. *Sam Walton*

Just having satisfied customers isn't good enough anymore. If you really want a booming business, you have to create raving fans. *Ken Blanchard*

Your most unhappy customers are your greatest source of learning. *Bill Gates*

Excellent customer service is the number one job in any company! It is the personality of the company and the reason customers come back. Without customers there is no company! *Connie Elder*

People do not care how much you know until they know how much you care. *Teddy Roosevelt*

Always have an attitude of gratitude. *James R. Nowlin*

Customer service should not be a department. It should be the entire company. *Tony Hsieh*

Value-added promotes customer retention (they come back) but value-unique nurtures customer advocacy (they bring their friends). *Chip Bell, Keynote Speaker & Author*

A customer is the most important visitor on our premises. He is not dependent on us. We are dependent on him. He is not an interruption in our work; he is the purpose of it. We are not doing him a favor by serving him. He is doing us a favor by giving us the opportunity to serve him. *Mahatma Gandhi*

Remember not only to say the right thing in the right place, but far more difficult still, to leave unsaid the wrong thing at the tempting moment. *Benjamin Franklin*

Conflict

The fine and noble way to destroy a foe, is not to kill him; with kindness you may so change him that he shall cease to be so: then he's slain. *Charles Aleyn*

Love your enemies, do good to them which hate you. *Luke*

Let us never negotiate out of fear. But let us never fear to negotiate. *John F. Kennedy*

He who throws dirt loses ground.

Handling criticism: If it's untrue, disregard it; it it's unfair, keep from irritation; if it's ignorant, smile; if it's justified, learn from it.

Peace is not absence of conflict, it is the ability to handle conflict by peaceful means. *Ronald Reagan*

Conflict can destroy a man who hasn't spent time learning to deal with it.

Whenever you're in conflict with someone, there is one factor that can make the difference between damaging your relationship and deepening it. That factor is attitude. *William James*

Courage is what it takes to stand up and speak. Courage is also what it takes to sit down and listen. *Winston Churchill*

People will forget what you said, they will forget what you did, but they will never forget how you made the feel. *Maya Angelou*

A willingness to trust and openly listen to alternative ideas and views is essential for collaboration to be successful. *Dale Eilerman*

The better able team members are to engage, speak, listen, hear, interpret, and respond constructively, the more likely their teams are to leverage conflict rather than being leveled by it. *Runde and Flanagan*

Love is the only force capable of transforming an enemy into a friend. *Dr. Martin Luther King, Jr.*

If we can manage conflict constructively, we harness its energy for creativity and development. *Kenneth Kaye*

In a conflict, being willing to change allows you to move from a point of view to a viewing point — a higher more expansive place, from which you can see both sides. *Thomas Crum*

In the middle of a difficulty lies opportunity. *Alfred Einstein*

Kind words do not cost much. Yet they accomplish much. *Blaise Pascal*

Festivus Day Graphic

Appendix B: 2019 Social Media Image Size Guide

All dimensions given in pixels.

Facebook

Cover Photo: 851 x 315
Profile Image: 200 x 200
Shared Image: 1200 x 630
Shared Link: 1200 x 630
Event Image: 1920 x 1080
Video Thumbnail: 1200 x 675
Ad: 476 x 714

LinkedIn

Profile Image: 400 x 400
Background Image: 1584 x 396
Standard Logo: 400 x 400
Company Cover Image: 1536 x 768

YouTube

Channel Profile: 800 x 800
Channel Cover Photo: 2560 x 1440
Video Uploads: 1280 x 720

Instagram

Profile Image: 180 x 180
Photo Thumbnail: 161 x 161
Photo Size: 1080 x 1080
Video Stories: 750 x 1334
Landscape: 1080 x 566
Portrait: 1080 x 1350

Twitter

Header Photo: 1500 x 500
Profile Photo: 400 x 400 (displays at 200 x 200)
Timeline Photo: 1024 x 512
Tweet Deck Photos
Profile Photo: 73 x 73
Header Image: 520 x 260
Timeline Photo: 260 x 300

Pinterest

Profile Image: 280 x 280
Giraffe Pin: 600 x 1560
Pin Sizes: 600 x 900

Tumbler

Profile Image: 128 x 128
Image Posts: 500 x750

Google+

Profile Image: 250 x 250
Cover Image: 1084 x 610
Shared Image: 530 wide
Shared Link Image: 530 wide

Ello

Banner Image: 1800 x 1300
Profile Image: 340 x 340

SnapChat

Geofilter Image: 1080 x 1920

Chinese Social Media

WeChat
Profile Photo: 200 x 200
Article Preview Header: 900 x 500
Article Preview Thumbnail: 400 x 400 (displays at 200 x 200)
Article Inline Image: 400 wide x any height

Weibo
Cover Image: 920 x 300
Profile Picture: 200 x 200 (displays at 100 x 100)
Banner: 550 x 260
Instream: 120 x 120
Contest Preview: 288 x 288
Contest Picture: 640 x 640
Contest Poster: 570 wide
Prize Picture: 200 x 200

Appendix C: LINKS

Link Checker
For Chrome: https://chrome.google.com/webstore/detail/check-my-links/ojkcdipcgfaekbeaelaapakgnjflfglf?hl=en-GB (I know this is out of alpha order, but a good link deserves top billing, don't you think? ;)
Article Marketing Sites
http://goarticles.com/
http://internationalpractice.com/business/
http://thephantomwriters.com/index.php
http://www.articledashboard.com/
http://www.articlegarden.com/
http://www.articlesbase.com/
http://www.articleson.com/
http://www.sitepronews.com/
http://www.selfgrowth.com
http://marniemarcus.com/unplugged/facebook-ad-management/
http://www.isnare.com
http://www.ladypens.com/
http://www.promotionworld.com
http://wahm-articles.com
http://www.writeandpublishyourbook.com/magazine/
https://contributor.yahoo.com/signup.shtml
http://www.ezinearticles.com

Auto Responder Services
AWeber: www.aweber.com/
Constant Contact: www.constantcontact.com/
Robly: https://app.robly.com/invite?rc=f56a53fb2ad6910f3e83ebda
Your Mailing List Provider: www.yourmailinglistprovider.com/

Books and Movies
Complete Library of Entrepreneurial Wisdom by Ginger Marks: http://www.CLEWbook.com
A Pirate's Life in the Golden Age of Piracy by Robert Jacob: https://aerbook.com/maker/productcard-3988088-2893.html
Customer Service Skills for Success by Robert W Lucas: http://a.co/d/739PPNL
#Next Level Manners: Business Etiquette for Millennials by Rachel Isgar Ph.D.: http://a.co/cew7qB4
Presentational Skills for the Next Generation by Ginger Marks: http://www.amazon.com/dp/B005EA01QO

Greeting Card Companies
123Greetings: http://www.123greetings.com
American Greetings: http://www.americangreetings.com/
Blue Mountain: www.bluemountain.com/
Cyberkisses: http://www.cyberkisses.com/
Day Springs: www.dayspring.com/ecards/
Evite: www.evite.com
Hallmark: http://www.hallmark.com/
Jacquie Lawson: www.jacquielawson.com/
Just Wink: https://www.justwink.com/
Operation Write Home: http://operationwritehome.org/
Punchbowl Greetings: http://www.punchbowl.com/invitations/preview/5400a4b424e4b36a3e000029/5400a56bbf947f655a000111
Send Out Cards: www.sendoutcards.com/

Podcast Directories
Corante-Podcasting: http://podcasting.corante.com/ — Weblog with news and events related to podcasting.
Hipcast: http://www.hipcaStcom/ — Audio and video podcasting service. Includes news and on-line tour.
iTunes: http://blog.lextext.com/blog/_archives/2005/1/4/225172.html — The iTunes Store puts thousands of free podcasts at your fingertips.
Lextext.com: How to Podcast RIAA Music Under License — http://blog.lextext.com/blog/_archives/2005/1/4/225172.html — Discussion of legal ways to podcast music. [Podcast is 5.3 MB in size]
The Liberated Syndication Network: http://www.libsyn.com/ — Full featured service tailored specifically for media Self-publishing and podcasting. Price is based on usage, changing monthly if needed.
NPR: http://www.npr.org/rss/podcast/podcast_directory.php — Over 50 public radio stations and producers are working with NPR to bring you podcasting.
The Podcast Directory: http://www.podcastdirectory.com/ — Up to date and relevant podcast directory.
Podcasting News: http://www.podcastingnews.com/ — Information relating to podcasting, a podcast directory, and a user forum.
SkypeCasters: http://www.henshall.com/blog/archives/001056.html — Introducing instructions for SkypeCasting, the solution for podcasters to create audio recordings from interviews and conference calls using Skype.
Skype Forums: http://forum.skype.com/viewtopic.php?t=12788 — Recording a Skype Conversation–Discussion thread covering software, techniques, and legal tidbits.
Wikipedia: Podcast –http://en.wikipedia.org/wiki/Podcast — Encyclopedia entry covering basics of the topic.

Promotional Product Supply Companies
4imprint: https://www.4imprint.com/ — offers free samples
Build A Sign: http://www.buildasign.com/
CafePress: www.cafepress.com/
Crown Awards: https://www.crownawards.com/
iPrint: http://www.iprint.com

Appendix C: LINKS | 139

Judie Glenn Inc: www.judieglenninc.com — ask for Tracey Arehart
Northwest Territorial Mint: http://custom.nwtmint.com/
Overnight Prints: http://www.overnightprints.com/
PC/Nametag˙: http://www.pcnametag.com/
Promotional Products: www.promotionalproducts.org/ — Get free quotes from multiple vendors
Staples: www.StaplesPromotionalProducts.com
VistaPrint: www.Vistaprint.com
World Class Medals: http://www.worldclassmedals.com/
Zazzle: http://www.zazzle.com/custom/buttons

Quote Sources
Bartleby: http://www.bartleby.com/
Brainy Quote: http://www.brainyquote.com/quotes/keywords/resources.html
Leadership Now: http://www.leadershipnow.com/quotes.html
Quote Garden: http://www.quotegarden.com/index.html
Quoteland: http://www.quoteland.com/
The Quotations Page: http://www.quotationspage.com/
Think Exit: http://thinkexist.com/quotes/american_proverb/
Woopidoo!: http://www.woopidoo.com/

Stock Photos
Tiny Eye: http://www.tineye.com — Reverse image search
Alamy: http://www.alamy.com
Beinecke: http://beinecke.library.yale.edu/digitallibrary
Maps Download MrSid: http://memory.loc.gov/ammem/help/download_sid.html
Big Stock Photo: http://www.bigstockphoto.com
Bing: http://www.bing.com
Can Stock Photo: http://www.canstockphoto.com
CreStock: http://www.crestock.com
DepositPhotos: http://depositphotos.com
Digital Scriptorium: http://bancroft.berkeley.edu/digitalscriptorium — public domain
Dreamstime: https://www.dreamstime.com
EJ Photo: http://www.ejphoto.com — Nature photography
Flickr: https://www.flickr.com — Advanced Search (only search on commercial content etc.)
Fotolia: http://www.foltolia.com
Foto Search: http://www.fotosearch.com
Free Digital Photos: http://www.freedigitalphotos.net
Free Photo: http://www.freefoto.com/index.jsp
Getty: http://www.gettyimages.com/
Google: http://www.images.google.com — Use Advanced Search for Usage Rights, labeled with commercial w/modifications
Icon Finder: http://www.iconfinder.com/illustrations
iStockPhoto: http://www.iStockPhoto.com
Jupiter: http://www.jupiterimages.com
Library of Congress: http://www.loc.gov/index.html — American Memory and Prints and Photographs sections
Morguefile: http://morguefile.com
PhotoSpin: https://www.photospin.com/Default.asp?

Pixabay: http://pixabay.com/
Pixadus: http://pixdaus.com
RGB Stock: www.rgbstock.com — more than 95,000 high quality free stock photos, graphics for illustrations, wallpapers, and backgrounds
Scriptorium: http://www.scriptorium.columbia.edu/ public domain
Shutterstock: http://www.shutterstock.com
Stockxchg (FreeImages): http://www.sxc.hu/
ThinkStock Photos: http://www.thinkstockphotos.com/
Top Left Pixel: http://wvs.topleftpixel.com
Visipix: http://www.visipix.com — lots of Japanese art
Visual Photos: http://www.visualphotos.com
Watercolor Textures: https://lostandtaken.com/downloads/category/paint/watercolor-texture/
WebStockPro: http://www.webstockpro.com/
Wikimedia Commons: http://commons.wikimedia.org/wiki/Main_Page — Check images via languages
Wikipedia Public Domain List: http://en.wikipedia.org/wiki/Wikipedia:Public_domain_image_resources/ public domain
You Work for Them: http://www.youworkforthem.com

Teleconference Companies
What is: www.business.com/directory/telecommunications/business_solutions/conferencing/
Buyer's Guide: www.buyerzone.com/telecom_services/telecon_services/buyers_guide5.html
Free Conference: www.freeconference.com/
Teleconference Live: http://teleconference.liveoffice.com
Teleconferencing Services: www.teleconferencingservices.net/
Wholesale Conference Call: www.wholesaleconferencecall.com/
Yugma Desktop Sharing Software: http://vur.me/gmarks/Yugma/
Zoom: https://www.zoom.us

Virtual Assistant Companies
A Clayton's Secretary (Kathie M Thomas): http://vadirectory.net/
Collins Administrative Services (Tracy Collins): http://www.collins-admin.com
MJ Stern, VA: http://www.mjstern-va.com/ — Specializes in internet marketing
Streamline Your Marketing (Crystal Pina): http://www.streamlineyourmarketing.com
Virtual Freedom 4 You (Corrie Petersen): http://virtualfreedom4you.com/

Webinar Services
Adobe Acrobat Connect Pro: http://tryit.adobe.com/us/connectpro/universalvoice/?sdid=DNOSU
BrainShark: http://brainshark.com/
Cisco WebEx: http://webex.com/
ClickWebinar: http://www.clickwebinar.com/
DimDim: http://www.dimdim.com/
Elluminate: http://www.elluminate.com/Products/?id=3
Facebook Live: https://live.fb.com/
Freebinar: http://www.freebinar.com/
Free Conference Calling: http://www.freeconferencecalling.com/
Fuze: http://www.fuzemeeting.com/

GatherPlace: http://www.gatherplace.net/start/
Google+ Hangouts: https://plus.google.com/hangouts
GoToMeeting: https://www.gotomeeting.com/
GoToWebinar: http://www.gotomeeting.com/fec/webinar
IBM Lotus Unyte: https://www.unyte.net/
iLinc: http://www.ilinc.com/
Infinite Conference: http://www.infiniteconference.com/
InstantPresenter: http://www.instantpresenter.com/
Intercall: http://www.intercall.com/smb/
Mega Meeting: http://www.megameeting.com/professional.html
Microsoft Office Live Meeting: http://www.microsoft.com/on-line/officE-livE-meeting/buy.mspx
Nefsis: http://www.nefsis.com/
Peter Pan Birthday Club: http://www.sjbhealth.org/body_foundation.cfm?id=1875
ReadyTalk: http://www.readytalk.com/
Saba Centra: http://saba.com/
StageToWeb: http://www.stagetoweb.com/livE-event–webcasting.html
Tokbox: http://tokbox.com/
Video Seminar Live: http://www.videoseminarlive.com/
Wix: http://www.wix.com/
Yugma: https://www.yugma.com/
Zoho: http://www.zoho.com/meeting/

Appendix D: RESOURCES

1507kot — https://www.vectorstock.com/royalty-free-vectors/vectors-by_1507kot
Babble Baby Names — https://www.babble.com/baby-names/
Baby Name Wizard — http://www.babynamewizard.com/
Behind the Name — https://www.behindthename.com/
Family Emergency Plan — http://pgward.org/ep/wp-content/uploads/2008/03/pg1familyplanform.pdf
Names.org — https://www.names.org/
Random Acts of Kindness — RandomActsofKindness.org

Twitter Tools Resources

Courtesy of Buffer https://blog.bufferapp.com/free-twitter-tools

Analytics
1. Daily 14 — https://www.daily140.com/?ref=producthunt
2. My Top Tweet — https://mytoptweet.com/
3. SocialBro — http://www.socialbro.com/
4. Riffle — http://crowdriff.com/riffle/
5. Twitonomy — http://www.twitonomy.com/
6. Klout — https://klout.com/#/overview
7. SumAll — http://sumall.com/
8. SocialRank — https://www.socialrank.com/
9. Klear — http://klear.com/
10. Bluenod — http://bluenod.com/
11. Twitter account home — http://analytics.twitter.com/
12. Social Bearing — http://www.socialbearing.com/
13. Stats for Twitter — https://itunes.apple.com/us/app/stats-for-twitter/id984958311?ref=producthunt

Chat
14. Beatstrap — http://www.beatstrap.me/
15. TweetChat — http://www.tweetchat.com/
16. Chat Salad — http://chatsalad.com/
17. Twubs — http://twubs.com/twitter-chats
18. Nurph — http://nurph.com/
19. TwChat — http://twchat.com/

Discovery
20. Nuzzel — http://nuzzel.com/
21. BuzzSumo — http://buzzsumo.com/
22. Swayy — http://www.swayy.co/#content

23. Twipho — http://twipho.net/
24. Digg Deeper — http://blog.digg.com/post/91454524841/digg-deeper
25. The Latest — http://latest.is/
26. Twurly — http://twurly.org/
27. Filta — https://filta.io
28. Hash — http://thehash.today/?ref=producthunt
29. Brook — http://www.brookdaily.com/

Follow/Unfollow
30. Crowdfire — https://www.crowdfireapp.com/
31. ManageFlitter — http://manageflitter.com/
32. Tweepi — http://www.tweepi.com/
33. Unfollowers — https://unfollowers.com/
34. DoesFollow — http://doesfollow.com/
35. Commun.it — https://commun.it/quick_actions
36. T.U.N.S. — http://tuns.it/?ref=producthunt
37. Twindr — http://twindr.me/?ref=producthunt
38. Toolset.co — https://toolset.co/
39. Linkreaser — http://www.linkreaser.com/
40. FollowFly — http://followfly.co/

Hashtags
41. Rite tag — https://ritetag.com/
42. Hashtagify.me — http://hashtagify.me/
43. Seen — http://seen.co/
44. Tagboard — https://tagboard.com/

Images
45. Pablo — https://buffer.com/pablo
46. Spruce — https://buffer.com/pablo
47. Twitshot — http://www.twitshot.com/?ref=producthunt
48. Share As Image — https://shareasimage.com/
49. Finch — http://getfinch.es/

Mentioning & Monitoring
50. Warble — https://warble.co/
51. Keyhole — http://keyhole.co/
52. The One Million Tweetmap — http://onemilliontweetmap.com/
53. Twilert — https://www.twilert.com/
54. Mention — https://en.mention.com/
55. MentionMapp — http://mentionmapp.com/
56. Twazzup — http://twazzup.com/

Scheduling
57. Buffer — http://twazzup.com/
58. Hootsuite — http://hootsuite.com/
59. Sprout Social — http://sproutsocial.com/
60. Tweet4me — http://tweet4.me/

Timing
61. Followerwonk — https://t.co/wIhlmwNgGG
62. Tweriod — http://www.tweriod.com/

Trending
63. Trends24 — http://trends24.in/
64. Trendsmap — http://trendsmap.com/
65. iTrended — http://itrended.com/

Top Clients
66. Tweetdeck — https://tweetdeck.twitter.com/
67. YoruFukurou — https://sites.google.com/site/yorufukurou/home-en
68. Happy Friends — http://happy.smallpict.com/2014/06/24/gettingStartedWithHappyFriends.html
69. Twitterific — http://twitterrific.com/ios?ref=producthunt
70. Twitter Dashboard — https://dashboard.twitter.com/i/landing
71. Hash — https://thehash.today/

Miscellaneous Tools
72. Like Explorer — http://twbirthday.com/
73. Twitter Feed — http://twitterfeed.com/
74. TW Birthday — http://twbirthday.com/
75. Bio is Changed — http://bioischanged.com/
76. IFTTT — https://ifttt.com/
77. Zapier — http://zapier.com/
78. Be Present — http://mustbepresent.com/
79. SavePublishing — http://www.savepublishing.com/
80. GroupTweet — http://grouptweet.com/
81. Storify — https://storify.com/
82. Tweet Topic Explorer — http://tweettopicexplorer.neoformix.com/
83. Listen to Twitter — http://listentotwitter.com/?ref=producthunt
84. Thunderclap — https://www.thunderclap.it/?ref=producthunt
85. Periscope — https://www.periscope.tv/?ref=producthunt
86. Meerkat — https://meerkatapp.co/
87. Twitterfav — https://www.twitterfav.com/
88. Click to Tweet — http://coschedule.com/click-to-tweet
89. Bedazzle — http://bedazzle.gordn.org/?ref=producthunt
90. Pullquote — http://pullquote.com/?ref=producthunt
91. Who Tweeted It First — http://ctrlq.org/first/
92. Little Pork Chop — http://pork.io/?ref=producthunt
93. Hubbble — http://hubbble.co/?ref=producthunt
94. Nudge — http://getnudge.co/app
95. SocialHunt — http://www.socialhuntapp.com/
96. Twitter Bookmarks — http://bookmarks.jazzyapps.com/

About the Author

Having been a business owner for most of her adult life, operating a multi–million-dollar surgical clinic and a local barbecue take-out to list just a couple, have given Ginger Marks the insight needed to assist business owners from all walks of life.

Ginger is the owner of the Calomar, LLC which holds her DocUmeant family of companies. The various entities all work towards a common goal that just happens to be their tagline; "We Make YOU Look GOOD!" Her services include both publishing and digital design assistance. She is proud of the fact that she is able to give high quality, efficient service at a remarkably reasonable rate. It is for this reason she chose to list her publishing company in New York City while residing in Florida.

When Ginger decided to embark on a writing career it was of no surprise to her mother, who herself is a published author. Her love for the arts is what spurred her to hone her talents as a digital designer, offering services to business owners and authors alike.

DocUmeant.net offers editing and writing services; DocUmeantDesigns.com, as you would guess, focuses on designs ranging from websites to book covers and layouts to buttons and business stationary needs; while DocUmeantPublishing.com's focus was begun with the self-published author in mind. Now with ten years of experience in publishing she has built her success in the global community.

Ginger is a member of DesignFirms where she is a top-rated designer, SPANpro (Small Publishers Association of North America), IBPA (International Book Publishers Association), DBW (Digital Book World), and is on the board of FAPA as VP Communications (Florida Authors and Publishers Association).

Most recently, Ginger was awarded for her generous contribution to internet business while helping others achieve their goals in publishing and marketing. The Golden Mouse Award was presented to her by Women In e-Commerce on Oct 28, 2016. In 2012 she was awarded VIP membership to Covington's Who's Who and her publishing company, DocUmeant Publishing, was awarded the 2012 and 2016 New York Award in the Publishing Consultants and Services category by the U.S. Commerce Association (USCA). She recently won the 2015 & 16 Clearwater, FL Design Firm Award and has won book cover design awards and is a multiple award winner for her *Weird & Wacky Holiday Marketing Guide* from FAPA.

In her spare time, she loves to do crafts of all sorts and sing. And yes, she is a little wacky at times too which keeps her fun and inspiring. Ginger lives in Florida where she works side-by-side with her husband, Philip, who is VP Editing for DocUmeant Publishing.

To contact Ginger whether for publish, design, or interviews you may reach her at ginger.marks@documeantdesigns.com or at 727-565-2130.

Additional Works by Ginger Marks

Visit Ginger's Amazon Author Central for more information or to purchase her books.
https://www.amazon.com/Ginger-Marks/e/B005ECOWD0/

Companion Playbook for Weird & Wacky Holiday Marketing Guide ISBN-13: 978-1937801779	The companion Playbook for the Annual *Weird & Wacky Marketing Guide* l will assist you in planning and tracking your holiday marketing success using the tools, tips, and resources found in the *Weird & Wacky Holiday Marketing Guide*. • Easily plan and track your marketing • Organized by month • Room to write notes • Track your success • No expiration date! Start using any time. Print: $12.97 Available at Amazon.com
Presentational Skills for the Next Generation, Third Edition, Ginger Marks Print ISBN: 978-0-9788831-4-0 Digital ISBN: 978-0-9832122-7-0	Much has changed over the years in the public speaking arena. We have so many new and challenging tools at our disposal that we are no longer consigned to countless hours to travel from city to city to share our knowledge. The internet has opened the doors to people from all places and races. At the click of a button, you can share your information in many forms of multi-media. With the availability of hosting online conferences and collaborations in both text-only and A/V environments, as are offered by Skype Conference™, Hot Conference™ and desktop sharing applications such as Yugma™, as well as teleconferences, the modes and means are so plentiful that more and more savvy business owners are venturing into the public speaking arena. It is a well thought out, concise, instructional manual written in a manner that all can comprehend. Within the contents of this guide, you will learn the skills necessary to enable you to present your information in such a way that you will capture the attention and hearts of your eager audience. Available in Print $14.95 Also available in Digital $9.95

$2.99
Kindle Edition
DOWNLOAD:
http://a.co/d/5xP5Ds7

Back to Basics is a collection of articles designed to assist the new business owner to jump start their business or the seasoned profession to put the punch back into their chosen career. It begins with a two-part series on the Nuts and Bolts of Business Building and continues from there to the ever-important Marketing Basics. As marketing is an issue for each and every business owner no matter their business or circumstances this section is presented in three parts. This eBook comes in Kindle and PDF versions and at $2.99 it is a real bargain.

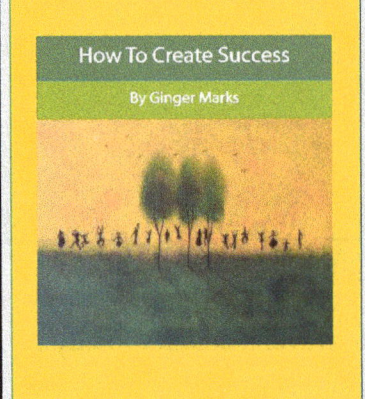

How To Create Success is the first eBook offering. Its bold colorful cover image entitled Jumping for Joy was designed by Amanda Tomasoa of Art by Amanda. The seven chapters contained within combine seven of the most highly rated articles written by Ginger at the time of publishing. One article Contagious Influence is currently the number one requested article and has been published in a magazine for writers titled 'Newbie News'. This is a free ebook and available for immediate download.

FREE to DOWNLOAD: http://www.gingermarksbooks.com/PDFs/HowToCreateSuccess.pdf.

To receive this FREE REPORT sign up for her monthly Words of Wisdom eZine at http://gingermarksbooks.com/.

In this report you will learn how to create an effective Long Sales Copy Web Page and why you might need one. As you read through this report if you come to the conclusion that a Long Sales Copy Web Page is the right tool for your business, I highly recommend you use the company or individual with the working knowledge and integrity to create the site you need to get your important message across to your target market.

If you haven't a clue how to decipher who your target market is then that it the best place to start. Without this knowledge, no matter how compelling your product or service message is, it will result in an ineffective campaign. This will end up costing you valuable time and money. Although this is beyond the context of this Special Report there are a myriad of resources available to you today online to help you along the way. As well, there are coaches who specialize in this area of expertise. Feel free to contact me and I will be happy to point you in the right direction.

	Discover the 10 truths every business owner should know. Knowing and applying these truths will aide you in achieving your dream of entrepreneurship. ©2008 Ginger Marks All rights reserved. To receive this eBook along with Ginger Marks' report *How to Create Long Sales Copy Web Pages* sign up for her monthly *Words of Wisdom eZine* at http://gingermarksbooks.com/.
 DOWNLOAD: http://clewbook.com/	Get your copy of Ginger's *Free Special Report: 10 Easy Steps to Re-purpose Your Content.* This is the insider's view of how the Complete Library of Entrepreneurial Wisdom came about. With the information you will garner in this Special Report, you too can quickly and easily create your very own new money maker.
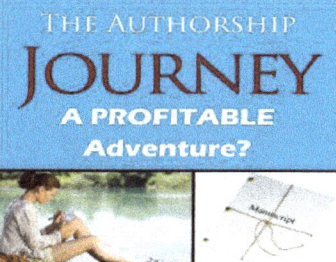 $0.99 Kindle Edition DOWNLOAD: http://a.co/d/3kRWOkf	The journey to authorship is a road few travel. Find out how you too can traverse the challenges that lie ahead and come out on top. Advice from leading experts in the field.

BUSINESS & PERSONAL GROWTH

Hardcover ISBN:
978-1937801380
Paperback ISBN:
978-1494928292

The Complete Library of Entrepreneurial Wisdom covers business basics, including how to and how not to start your business; marketing; marketing design, which is a topic rarely covered; writing, which covers technical, practical, as well as, marketing aspects to writing; and life reflections, such as planning for emergencies and disasters—both natural and man-made.

With over 150, power-packed, articles to choose from, the busy entrepreneur has at their fingertips, bite-sized training lessons to help them on their success journey. There is so much information packed into this book that it could well be the only book on core business issues that you will ever need.

$9.97 Kindle
$32.95 Hardcover
$24.95 Paperback

$2.99 Kindle Edition

Publishing your ebook on Kindle doesn't guarantee your book will look the way you intended it to. Even using the Kindle generation tools can result in an ebook that isn't laid out the way you created it. In *Kindle Publishing, Yes You Can,* Ginger Marks, publisher and designer, explains in easy terms exactly what you need to do and how to create an ebook on Kindle that you will be proud to call your own.

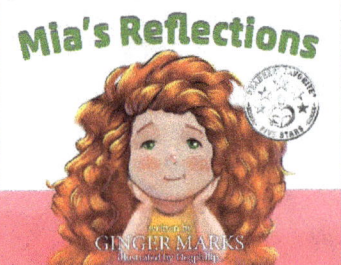

$6.99 Kindle Edition
$14.99 Print Edition
(Feb 2019)

Ginger's first children's picture book, *Mia's Reflections* captures the heart of a young girl who learns that beauty is not just a pretty face, but rather a giving life.

Anticipating a new school with no friends, where she feels alone and ugly, young Mia prepares for her first day. She steps near her Grandmother's old Cheval mirror and there she senses her mama reaching out to her. "You're not ugly," her mama says. "You're beautiful." And she traces all the beautiful services Mia performs in a day. At last her mother appears in the mirror to give a fresh look at Mia's loveliness.

Followed by Parent/Teacher resources, this book will fill a young girl's day with thoughts of love and kindness.

Book trailer: https://youtu.be/4DoQe9zp8LY

Weird & Wacky Holiday Marketing Guide
Complete Your Collection Today!

Previous Editions Available here: http://www.HolidayMarketingGuide.com/past.html

Previous Editions Available at HolidayMarketingGuide.com/past.html
Affiliate Marketing Opportunities available at http://www.HolidayMarketingGuide.com!

www.ingramcontent.com/pod-product-compliance
Lightning Source LLC
Chambersburg PA
CBHW080920170426
43201CB00016B/2206